EL ESSENTIALS

— ⁄⁄ ON ⁄⁄ —

Being a Teacher

EL ESSENTIALS

ON

Being a Teacher

Readings from
Educational Leadership

Edited by
Marge Scherer

ASCD
Alexandria, VA USA

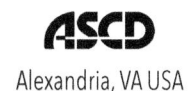

1703 N. Beauregard St. • Alexandria, VA 22311-1714 USA
Phone: 800-933-2723 or 703-578-9600 • Fax: 703-575-5400
Website: www.ascd.org • E-mail: member@ascd.org
Author guidelines: www.ascd.org/write

Deborah S. Delisle, *Executive Director*; Robert D. Clouse, *Managing Director, Digital Content & Publications*; Stefani Roth, *Publisher*; Genny Ostertag, *Director, Content Acquisitions*; Julie Houtz, *Director, Book Editing & Production*; Julie Huggins, *Editorial Assistant*; Thomas Lytle, *Senior Graphic Designer*; Mike Kalyan, *Manager, Production Services*; Cynthia Stock, *Production Designer*; Andrea Wilson, *Senior Production Specialist*

Educational Leadership Staff
Margaret M. Scherer, *Editor in Chief*; Deborah Perkins-Gough, *Senior Editor*; Kim Greene, *Senior Associate Editor*; Naomi Thiers, *Associate Editor*; Lucy Robertson, *Associate Editor*; Judi Connelly, *Associate Art Director*

Copyright © 2016 ASCD. All rights reserved. It is illegal to reproduce copies of this work in print or electronic format (including reproductions displayed on a secure intranet or stored in a retrieval system or other electronic storage device from which copies can be made or displayed) without the prior written permission of the publisher. By purchasing only authorized electronic or print editions and not participating in or encouraging piracy of copyrighted materials, you support the rights of authors and publishers. Readers who wish to reproduce or republish excerpts of this work in print or electronic format may do so for a small fee by contacting the Copyright Clearance Center (CCC), 222 Rosewood Dr., Danvers, MA 01923, USA (phone: 978-750-8400; fax: 978-646-8600; web: www.copyright.com). To inquire about site licensing options or any other reuse, contact ASCD Permissions at www.ascd.org/permissions, or permissions@ascd.org, or 703-575-5749. For a list of vendors authorized to license ASCD e-books to institutions, see www.ascd.org/epubs. Send translation inquiries to translations@ascd.org.

All referenced trademarks are the property of their respective owners.

All web links in this book are correct as of the publication date below but may have become inactive or otherwise modified since that time. If you notice a deactivated or changed link, please e-mail books@ascd.org with the words "Link Update" in the subject line. In your message, please specify the web link, the book title, and the page number on which the link appears.

PDF E-BOOK ISBN: 978-1-4166-2228-4   ASCD product #116063E4   n6/16
See Books in Print for other formats.
Quantity discounts: 10–49, 10%; 50+, 15%; 1,000+, special discounts (e-mail programteam@ascd.org or call 800-933-2723, ext. 5773, or 703-575-5773). For desk copies, go to www.ascd.org/deskcopy.

23 22 21 20 19 18 17 16   1 2 3 4 5 6 7 8 9 10 11 12

EL ESSENTIALS

— // ON //—

Being a Teacher

Introduction: The Most Influential Teachers by Marge Scherer 1

1. Eight Things Skilled Teachers Think, Say, and Do by Larry Ferlazzo 3
   When students test you—and they will—do what the master teachers do.

2. The Don'ts and Don'ts of Teaching by Gary Rubinstein. 12
   Here's one writer's list of behaviors to actively avoid.

3. Notes from an Accidental Teacher by Carol Ann Tomlinson. 19
   On your journey to become an effective teacher, consider these five professional practices that will help you find your way.

4. New Teachers Face Three Challenges by Bryan Goodwin 28
   New teachers bring energy and enthusiasm to their classrooms, but also a specific set of needs.

5. Essential Skills for New Teachers by H. Jerome Freiberg. 33
   On-the-job training for novice teachers must include planning, management, and assessment techniques.

6. The Challenges of Supporting New Teachers:
   A Conversation with Linda Darling-Hammond by Marge Scherer 42
   Researcher Linda Darling-Hammond reflects on the promising practices and the significant obstacles that face beginning teachers.

7. Ten Roles for Teacher Leaders by Cindy Harrison and Joellen Killion 54
   From instructional specialist to committee chair, teachers in these roles can change the status quo.

8. Why Teachers Must Become Change Agents by Michael G. Fullan 61
   To have any chance of making teaching a noble and effective profession, teachers must combine the mantle of moral purpose with the skills of change agents.

9. The Problem-Solving Power of Teachers by Ariel Sacks 73
   Too many education issues have yet to truly benefit from teachers' ideas.

10. Take Back Teaching Now by Nancy Flanagan 83
    Before educators can become change agents, they must reclaim their professional courage.

11. Teaching Is Leading by Michelle Collay 91
    Effective teaching requires everyday acts of leadership.

12. Now That I Know What I Know by Dan Brown........................100
    What a teacher learned from a power struggle with a student.

13. Edcamp: Teachers Take Back Professional Development
    by Kristen Swanson 109
    The Edcamp experience empowers teachers to share their best ideas.

14. The Best Teachers I Have Known by Susan Allred 117
    Whether they were teaching in the 1960s or in the 2000s, effective teachers share a common set of characteristics.

Study Guide by Naomi Thiers..123
   Ideas to try out individually or in a study group.

EL Takeaways: On Being a Teacher 127

Introduction
The Most Influential Teachers

If you had to name the defining characteristic of a "good teacher," what trait would you suggest? Would you start ticking off the characteristics listed on the evaluation framework used in your district? If so, you might note "content knowledge," "managing classroom environments," "communicating with students," or "reflecting on teaching."

Or would you think back to your own experiences and consider the most memorable educators you've known? What one characteristic do "the best of all your good teachers" have in common? When I do this, I think of Mother Bascomb, a college professor who knew *The Canterbury Tales* so well she could recite them in middle English. (The word *expertise* comes to mind.) And I think of Ramanan, a yoga teacher who humored his class into daily practice by assigning "easy homework." (The word here is *humor.*) Or should I consider my otherwise unpopular 8th grade teacher who memorably wrote on my paper, "You will be a writer someday." (The word is *supportive.*) As I think back, these outlier "good teachers" had vastly different qualities that made them exceptional.

In this collection of articles, our authors—all educators and educators of educators—discuss from different points of view and in different styles what it means to be a good teacher. Pulled from *Educational Leadership* issues that over the years have featured such themes as

"The Effective Educator," "Teachers as Leaders," and "Supporting Good Teachers," these articles include tips and strategies for everything from connecting with students to planning the teaching day (Ferlazzo, Rubinstein, Brown, Allred); reflections on the profession as a whole—how it is changing and where it is going (Freiberg, Darling-Hammond, Fullan, and Harrison and Killion); and descriptions of practices that can make the teaching experience more effective and more rewarding (Tomlinson, Goodwin, Sacks, Flanagan, and Collay).

In choosing these articles for you, the editors of *Educational Leadership* looked for the most practical and timeless pieces. Our purpose was to bring to your fingertips articles you may have missed the first time around or would enjoy rereading and sharing with fellow educators. This collection is especially designed for new teachers who need words of wisdom and support; experienced teachers and teacher leaders who want to reflect on their practice and expand their influence; study groups and classes exploring the essentials of good teaching; and principals and coaches who want to give their staff or colleagues a collection of materials that will remind them of why they went into teaching in the first place.

Quite a long time ago, Henry Adams wrote that teachers "affect a kind of immortality" because they "never can tell where their influence stops." We hope these articles inspire you to celebrate good teachers everywhere as well as become the best teacher you can be.

—Marge Scherer
Editor in Chief, *Educational Leadership*

Eight Things Skilled Teachers Think, Say, and Do

Larry Ferlazzo

When students test you—and they will—do what the master teachers do.

Among the many challenges teachers face, often the most difficult is how to engage students who seem unreachable, who resist learning activities, or who disrupt them for others. This is also one of the challenges that skilled teachers have some control over. In my nine years of teaching high school, I've found that one of the best approaches to engaging challenging students is to develop their intrinsic motivation.

The root of intrinsic is the Latin *intrinsecus*, a combination of two words meaning *within* and *alongside*. It's likely that our students *are* intrinsically motivated—just motivated to follow their own interests, not to do what we want them to do. Teachers' challenge is to work alongside our students, to know their interests and goals, and to develop trusting relationships that help students connect their learning to their goals in a way that motivates from within.

How can teachers do this? It's helpful to consider this question in three parts: What skilled teachers think, what they say, and what they do.

What Skilled Teachers Can Think

What we think guides how we view the world, including how we view challenging students. Developing and maintaining three mind-sets will help teachers maintain their equilibrium in the face of behavior or resistance to learning from certain students that would ordinarily knock us off balance.

1. Remember that authoritative beats authoritarian.
Being authoritarian means wielding power unilaterally to control someone, demanding obedience without giving any explanation for why one's orders are important. Being authoritative, on the other hand, means demonstrating control, but doing so relationally through listening and explaining. Studies of effective parenting have found that children view parents who use an authoritative style as legitimate authority figures; such children are less likely to engage in delinquent behavior. The opposite is true for children of authoritarian parents (University of New Hampshire, 2012).

It's not too much of a stretch to apply this finding to teachers and students. As you interact with students, frequently ask yourself which of these two styles you use. Do you want to always lead with your mouth—or with your ears? Bring this authoritative-authoritarian question to bear on your classroom practices. In terms of instruction, are you always the sage on stage? Do you have students periodically evaluate your class and you as a teacher—and seriously consider their feedback? Do you explain to students why you teach the way you do? When a student's behavior is causing a problem, do you control the behavior at any cost, or do you try to find out what's going on with that student? Opting for the authoritative style will make students more likely to respect your authority—and probably more eager to cooperate.

2. Believe that everyone can grow.
Many teachers are familiar with Carol Dweck's distinction between a "growth" mind-set and a "fixed" one. When we have a growth mind-set,

we believe that everyone has the inner power to grow and change. We see mistakes as opportunities to learn. Holding a fixed mind-set leads us to believe that people's traits—such as intelligence—are immutable. A mistake on the part of someone we believe is unintelligent seems to validate that belief.

Which mind-set we hold makes a tremendous difference. In one study, a researcher measured teachers' mind-sets at the beginning of the year. In classes led by teachers who showed fixed mind-sets, few students with learning challenges advanced academically during the year. But in classes taught by those with growth mind-sets, many previously low-performing students made gains (Dweck, 2010). Teachers with a fixed mind-set tend to immediately and permanently place students into categories. They place the primary responsibility for overcoming learning challenges on the students. Those with a growth mind-set consider responding to a student's challenges to be the joint responsibility of the student and the educator.

Teachers aren't superhuman. There are some things we cannot accomplish. But we must ask ourselves whether we too readily write off students who try our patience as "incapable," or some similar adjective, without considering whether differentiating instruction for these students might spur change and growth.

One of my students had never written an essay in his school career. He was intent on maintaining that record during our unit on writing persuasive essays. Because I knew two of his passions were football and video games, I told him that as long as he used the writing techniques we'd studied, he could write an essay on why his favorite football team was better than its rival or on why he particularly liked one video game. He ended up writing an essay on both topics.

3. Understand that power isn't a finite pie.
I was a community organizer for 19 years before I became a teacher. A key lesson I learned was that power isn't a finite pie. If I share the power

I have, that doesn't mean I'll have less. In fact, the pie will get bigger as more possibilities are created for everyone.

Power struggles are at the root of much misbehavior. William Glasser (1988) believes that students have a basic need for power and that 95 percent of classroom management issues occur as a result of students trying to fulfill this need. Having more power actually helps students learn. Giving students choices—about their homework, assignments, how they're grouped, and so on—leads to higher levels of student engagement and achievement (Sparks, 2010).

Remembering that power isn't finite helps us see that asking students for ideas on what might help them feel more engaged isn't a sign of weakness, but of strength. So is seeking advice from students' parents or from teachers in other classes in which challenged learners show more success. Over the years, I've gained great insight and become a more effective teacher by asking parents, "Tell me about a time in your child's life when he or she was learning a lot and working hard in school. What was his or her teacher doing then?"

What Skilled Teachers Can Say

4. Give positive messages.
Positive messages are essential to motivation. Subtle shifts in teacher language infuse positive messages throughout our interactions. Here are three practices I've found helpful.

Use positive framing. "Loss framed" messages (if you do this, then something bad will happen to you) don't have the persuasive advantage that they're often thought to have. "Positive framed" messages (if you do this, these good things will happen) are more effective (Dean, 2010). I've had more success talking with students about how changing their behavior will help them achieve their goals (such as graduating from high school or going to college) than I've had threatening them with negative consequences. Positive messages that connect students' current actions to broader student-identified hopes or goals are different from "if-then" statements focused on what teachers want students to do ("If you don't get out of your seat without permission, then you'll get extra credit"). As Daniel Pink (2009) notes, such extrinsic manipulations don't develop students' higher-order thinking skills or long-term commitments to change.

Say "yes." Avoidant instruction is language that emphasizes what people should not do ("Don't walk on the grass." "Don't chew gum"). Some researchers (British Psychological Society, 2010) believe that a more effective way to get a desired behavior is to emphasize what you want people to do. For example, if a student asks to go the restroom, but the timing isn't right, rather than saying no, I try to say, "Yes, you can. I just need you to wait a few minutes." Or if a student is talking at an inappropriate time, instead of saying, "Don't talk!" I sometimes go over and tell that learner, "I see you have a lot of energy today. We'll be breaking into small groups later and you'll have plenty of time to talk then. I'd appreciate your listening now."

Say "please" and "thank you." People are more likely to comply with a task (and do so more quickly) if someone asks them instead of tells them (Yong, 2010). I've found that "Can you please sit down?" is more effective than "Sit down!" Saying thank you provides immediate positive reinforcement to students. Research (Sutton, 2010) shows that people who are thanked by authority figures are more likely to cooperate, feel valued, and exhibit self-confidence.

5. Apologize.

Teachers are human, and we make plenty of mistakes. There is no reason why we shouldn't apologize when we do.

But saying, "I'm sorry," may not be enough. I often use the "regret, reason, and remedy" formula recommended by Dorothy Armstrong (2009). For example, one afternoon my students Omar and Quang were paired up in my class but were sitting passively while everyone else focused on the task at hand. I said sharply, "Come on now, get working!" A few minutes later, I said simply to the two boys, "I'm sorry I barked at you earlier. I was frustrated that you weren't doing what I'd asked you to do. I'll try to show more patience in the future." They clearly focused more energy on their work after this apology.

What Skilled Teachers Can Do

6. Be flexible.
Being flexible might be the most important thing teachers can "do" to help students who challenge us—in fact all students—to get past whatever challenges of their own they confront. Three practices help me differentiate instruction and classroom management in a way that helps everyone.

Help them get started. Psychologist Bluma Zeigarnik identified the Zeigarnik Effect: Once people start doing something, they tend to want to finish it (Dean, 2011). If we get a disengaged or anxious student started, that's half the battle. For a task that's likely to challenge some students, present a variety of ways to get started: a menu of questions, the option to create a visual representation of a concept, a chance to work with a partner. Encourage students to launch themselves by just answering the first question or the easiest one.

Help postpone tempting distractions. Making a conscious decision to postpone giving in to temptation can reduce a desire that's getting in the way of a goal (Society for Personality and Social Psychology, 2012). My student Mai was frequently using her cell phone to text message during class. I didn't want to take her phone away, so I made a deal with her—she could text in my classroom during two specific times: from the moment she entered the room until the bell rang and as soon as the lunch bell rang. Since we made that deal, Mai hardly ever uses her cell phone during class. Even more significant, she hardly ever uses it during our agreed-on times.

Acknowledge stress. As most of us know from experience, people tend to have less self-control when they're under stress (Szalavitz, 2012). When a student is demonstrating self-control issues in my class, I often learn through a conversation with him or her that this student is going through family disruptions or similar problems. Sometimes, just providing students an opportunity to vent worries can have a positive effect.

7. Set the right climate.
Pink (2009) and other researchers have found that extrinsic rewards work in the short term for mechanical tasks that don't require much higher-order thinking, but they don't produce true motivation for work that requires higher-order thinking and creativity. However, everyone needs "baseline rewards"—conditions that provide adequate compensation for one's presence and effort.

At school, baseline rewards might include fair grading, a caring teacher, engaging lessons, and a clean classroom. If such needs aren't met, Pink (2009) notes, the student will focus on "the unfairness of her situation and the anxiety of her circumstance. … You'll get neither the predictability of extrinsic motivation nor the weirdness of intrinsic motivation. You'll get very little motivation at all" (p. 35).

8. Teach life lessons.
My colleagues and I frontload our school year with what we call life-skills lessons.[1] These simple, engaging activities help students see how it's in their short-term and long-term interest to try their best.

For example, a lesson might highlight how the learning process physically alters the brain. This particular lesson encourages a growth mind-set. It was eye-opening to one of my students who had claimed, "We're all born smart or dumb and stay that way." In terms of keeping up kids' motivation, the times throughout the year when I refer back to these concepts and reflect on how they apply to learning struggles are as important as the initial lessons.

What We Can Always Do

Consistently implementing these practices is easier said than done—and is probably impossible unless you're Mother Teresa. But most teachers already do something that makes all these practices flow more naturally, and that we can do more intensely with conscious effort—we build relationships with students. Caring relationships with teachers helps students build resilience. By fostering these relationships, we learn about students' interests and goals, which are fuel for motivation.

On Fridays, my students write short reflections about the week. One Friday, I asked them to write about the most important thing they'd learned in class that week. One student wrote, "I didn't really learn anything important this week, but that's OK because Mr. Ferlazzo tried his best."

Although I wasn't that thrilled with the first part of his comment, there's an important message in the second half. Even if we can't always think, say, and do the ideal thing to strengthen struggling students' motivation, there's always something we can do to meet them halfway. We can try our best.

Endnote

[1] Lesson plans are available free at my blog.

References

Armstrong, D. (2009). The power of apology: How saying sorry can leave both patients and nurses feeling better. *Nursing Times*, 105(44), 16–19.

British Psychological Society. (2010, October 13). Don't touch! On the mixed effects of avoidant instructions [blog post]. Retrieved from *Research Digest* at http://bps-research-digest.blogspot.com/2010/10/dont-touch-on-mixed-effects-of-avoidant.html

Dean, J. (2010, December 1). The influence of positive framing [blog post]. Retrieved from *Psyblog* at www.spring.org.uk/2010/12/the-influence-of-positive-framing.php

Dean, J. (2011, February 8). The Zeigarnik effect [blog post]. Retrieved from *PsyBlog* at www.spring.org.uk/2011/02/the-zeigarnik-effect.php

Dweck, C. S. (2010, January). Mind-sets and equitable education. *Principal Leadership*, *10*(5), 26–29. Retrieved from www.principals.org/Content.aspx?topic=61219

Glasser, W. (1988b). On students' needs and team learning: A conversation with William Glasser. *Educational Leadership, 45*(6), 38–45.

Pink, D. (2009). *Drive.* New York: Riverhead Books.

Society for Personality and Social Psychology. (2012, January 30). Willpower and desires: Turning up the volume on what you want most. *Science Daily.*

Sparks, S. D. (2010, December 21). Giving students a say may spur engagement and achievement [blog post]. Retrieved from *Education Week: Inside School Research* at http://blogs.edweek.org/edweek/inside-school-research/2010/12/class_choice_may_spur_student.html

Sutton, B. (2010, August 28). It isn't just a myth: A little thanks goes a long way [blog post]. Retrieved from *Work Matters* at http://bobsutton.typepad.com/my_weblog/2010/08/it-isnt-just-a-myth-a-little-thanks-goes-a-long-way.html

Szalavitz, M. (2012, March 5). Decision making under stress: The brain remembers rewards, forgets punishments. *Time.* Retrieved from http://healthland.time.com/2012/03/05/decision-making-under-stress-the-brain-remembers-rewards-forgets-punishments

University of New Hampshire (2012, February 10). Controlling parents more likely to have delinquent children. *Science Daily.*

Yong, E. (2010, March 19). Requests work better than orders, even when we're asking or ordering ourselves [blog post]. Retrieved from *Science Blogs: Not Exactly Rocket Science.*

Larry Ferlazzo (MrFerlazzo@aol.com) teaches English and social studies at Luther Burbank High School in Sacramento, California. He is coauthor, with Katie Hull Sypnieski, of *The ESL/ELL Teacher's Survival Guide* (Jossey-Bass, 2012).

Originally published online in the October 2012 issue of *Educational Leadership, 70*(2).

The Don'ts and Don'ts of Teaching

Gary Rubinstein

Here are 10 mistakes a rookie should avoid.

One piece of advice that I've seen in numerous books about teaching is to always phrase classroom rules positively. Instead of phrasing a rule as "no talking," for instance, teachers should phrase it as "talk in turn." The theory, I suppose, is that when students are told not to do one thing without being told what they should do instead, they may not know their options. Proponents also argue that phrasing rules in the positive is less confrontational; rebellious students will be less apt to break a positively stated procedure than a negatively worded rule.

I don't buy this. For new teachers, especially, classroom rules need to be rules, and a rule should be stated in the clearest way possible. Many of the most important rules adults have to abide by are written in the negative: No parking. No dogs allowed. Do not disturb. Do not pass go. Do not collect 200 dollars. Thou shalt not kill.

The same books that suggest this positive approach to rule making often take a similar approach to the rules they suggest new teachers should abide by. But just as it's wrong to be too subtle when instructing children, it's wrong to be too subtle when instructing new teachers.

This is particularly true when the teachers are trained through a crash-course alternative certification program.

As a product of the second-ever Teach for America institute back in the summer of 1991, I was taught the essentials of teaching in this indecisive way. As a new teacher, my classroom performance suffered partly because of this lack of clarity. I was told that there are many correct ways to do something. Although this is true, there are also many wrong ways to do something. Rookie teachers, who struggle to sort out right ways from wrong, would be better served by a clear list of behaviors to actively avoid.

I made all the mistakes I describe here in my first year of teaching. As nobody clearly warned me about these mistakes, I had to learn for myself through trial and error. Unfortunately, by the time I realized that I'd made these blunders, I'd already lost my students' respect. It was too late to convince them that I knew what I was doing.

Sherlock Holmes always maintained, "Eliminate all other factors, and the one which remains must be the truth." We can apply this principle to teaching: It's a lot more efficient to learn a few mistakes that you should avoid than to learn all the things you should do right. When I compare my awful first year with my very successful second year, the main difference was not so much what I did as what I *didn't* do. Here are 10 rookie teacher mistakes I wish I'd avoided.

1. Don't try to teach too much in one day.

This is an easy mistake to make because it's intertwined with another rule for new teachers: Have high expectations. Of course teachers should always expect students to do their best. But the oversold exhortation to "have high expectations" needs further explanation. If it were only that easy, every teacher would be hugely successful.

New teachers, particularly those without extensive student teaching, take this advice too literally and create lessons that are too difficult, too long, or developmentally inappropriate. Even as a veteran teacher, I still often attempt to do too much in one day. It comes from my desire to not bore students by doing too little.

But the risks of overpacking a class period are too high; better to split a lesson originally planned for one day into a two-day affair. If you rush your lesson, it might not be received well by students. Then you'll have to spend the next day doing the dreaded reteaching.

2. Don't teach a lesson without a student activity.

One problem new teachers have is that they think they need to plan each lesson "chronologically." First they plan their opening exercises, then their direct instruction and classroom discussion questions, and, finally, their activity. The problem is that they frequently spend so much time thinking about all the great things they're going to say in their direct lesson that they use up their planning time—or fall asleep—before creating the most important, most time-consuming, component. I advise new teachers to always plan their activity first, even if it's the last thing that will occur. We can wing direct instruction and discussion if necessary but not a thoughtful learning activity.

When a lesson has no activity, students get restless and tune out. And I find I'm more enthusiastic and efficient with direct instruction when I know I have a great activity coming right after my instruction.

3. Don't send kids to the office.

No matter how many times a principal says, "just send them to me," it's not a good idea. When you send kids out, it soon becomes the only thing they'll respond to. In some schools, the office is nothing more than a place where disruptive kids hang out with one another. In my first teaching year, I intercepted a note that said, "Get sent to the office 6th period. I'll meet you there."

"So," you might be thinking now, "what *should* I do when students are misbehaving?" I have no pat answers about the complex question of how to handle challenging behavior, but I do know that if you avoid the mistakes I mention here, you won't have as many discipline problems. And, unfortunately, if you do make these mistakes, anything you try to do to fix your discipline problems will be as ineffective as sending kids to the office.

4. Don't allow students to shout out answers.

Watch any current movie about a transformational teacher and you'll notice the lively discussions that go on in her class. She'll pose a question. One student will call out a poignant response, another will chime in, and then yet another. These scenarios could make a novice teacher feel that in a well-run classroom students don't need to raise their hands to make comments.

But novice teachers need to know that it takes a fictional teacher-hero or heroine to get away with letting students call out. Other students in the class often zone out when they know there's no chance that the teacher will call on them, so what feels like a class buzzing with discussion is really just a few kids speaking up while the rest pretend to listen. Instead, expert teachers pose thoughtful questions, wait for plenty of hands to go up, and then call on a volunteer—or even a nonvolunteer.

5. Don't make tests too hard.

Although teachers use tests to gauge how well students are learning, students often use a test to gauge how well the teacher is teaching. If you accidentally—or purposely—make a test too hard, neither thing will be accurately measured. You might realize that the students underperformed on your too-difficult test, but students might just assume that you didn't teach well. This will make them less enthusiastic about learning from you.

When I finish making a test, I often cut out about 25 percent of the test to make it more manageable. One way to do this is to assign a priority level of 1, 2, or 3 to each question, with 1 being high priority and 3 lower priority. Then you can keep all the 1s and cut all the 3s. Kids are not insulted by an "easy" test. It gives them confidence.

6. Don't be indecisive.

Although this could certainly be phrased more positively ("be decisive"), I phrased it this way to emphasize that teachers must actively avoid indecisive behavior. When a student asks a question like, "Can I do my test in red ink?" you have three seconds to pause, consider the question, and answer *yes* or *no*. There is no wrong answer, only a wrong way of saying it.

If you conclude you've made a bad decision, it's possible to reverse it the next day. Even your reversal, however, must be done decisively: "I thought that, but now I think this. Let's move on."

7. Don't tell a student you're calling home.

When you've decided, in your mind, that you've had enough, keep that information to yourself. Calling home is one of the best things you can do to respond to student misbehavior, but it must always be a surprise.

When you warn a student you're calling home, that student often increases his misbehavior because he wants his classmates to think that he doesn't care, even if he does. Also, if you warn a student, she will get a chance to intercept your call, warn her parent, or distort the facts. Finally, you'll look like someone who can't follow through on a threat if, for whatever reason, you are unable to reach the parent that evening.

8. Don't try to be a buddy.

Another mistake we learn from inspirational movies is that to get through to certain kids, you've got to be their buddy. Although all teacher training programs warn about the problems with trying to be a student's friend, it is still a common new teacher mistake.

New teachers may follow the prohibition in the beginning of the year but let up on it way too soon, when things are going well. I suggest you mark on the calendar a random day, some day in February, to be the first time you carefully cross the buddy line for a short visit before returning back.

9. Don't dress too casually.

New teachers often intentionally dress so that they don't look like the typical teacher, believing that a traditional looking teacher will have trouble reaching certain kids. A new teacher with a casual personal style outside the schoolhouse may genuinely believe, "If I'm not myself, these kids will pick up on it immediately." I disagree. If you look like a teacher, they will treat you like a teacher. Not appearing like a professional is way too big a risk.

10. Don't babble.

New teachers are usually nervous, and nervous people often babble. The more words you say, the less value each word has. I once heard that teachers get to say about 10,000 words before the students stop listening, and that new teachers use up their words in the first week. Choose your words carefully.

Fewer Mistakes = More Learning

The urgency of avoiding mistakes is stronger in teaching than in most professions. The only profession where it's more difficult to salvage your mistakes is tightrope walking. Because we deal with students, who hold on to first impressions, teachers don't get to start over with a fresh slate after making numerous mistakes, the way a waiter might.

Being aware of these 10 mistakes doesn't mean that you'll never make them. Even after 20 years of teaching, I still struggle daily to avoid these blunders. But every mistake you avoid will lead to a better learning experience for your students. As teachers, we might learn from our mistakes. Our students won't.

Gary Rubinstein (garyrubinstein@yahoo.com) teaches math at Stuyvesant High School in New York City. He is the author of *Beyond Survival* (McGraw-Hill, 2010).

Originally published in the May 2012 issue of *Educational Leadership, 69*(8): pp. 50–52.

Notes from an Accidental Teacher

Carol Ann Tomlinson

What builds a solid teacher? The right setting, a sense of calling, a zeal for learning, and a renewable energy source.

I've always liked the title of Anne Tyler's book *The Accidental Tourist*, perhaps because much of my life—and certainly my teaching career—seems accidental. I'd love to say that I never wanted to be anything but a teacher. In truth, I aspired *not* to be a teacher.

My mother was a teacher—a very strong one. For one year in my early adolescence, I went to the school where she taught. It was a dismal year for me. I was the new kid in my class, having just moved with my parents from another town. I was too tall for 6th grade. My hair was too long (until I made an argument for getting it cut, and then it was too short, too straight, and too stubborn). The school was very different from my prior school, and I couldn't quite figure it out. I was pathologically shy.

The teachers in the school were good people and good educators. That made no difference. From time to time, a teacher would say something to my mom about me and the comment would innocently make its way into dinner-table talk at home. I hated the feeling of being watched and talked about. I vowed with rancorous fervor that I would never under any circumstances be a teacher.

I didn't major in education in college. My first job out of college was stultifying and had nothing to do with teaching. One Friday in late October, finding the morning at work to be particularly tedious, I read the want ads in the local paper at lunch. There was a teaching vacancy in a town an hour away that I had never heard of. I took the afternoon off, applied for the job, and began teaching the following Monday.

To say that I didn't know what I was doing when I entered the classroom redefines the word *understatement*. I planned to finish out the year in that little rural school and then get a "real" job. That was four decades ago, and I've never since had the inclination to do anything but teach.

Nonetheless, my career evolved—as it began—more by happenstance than by design. Teaching works for me, my work is satisfying, and I feel proud—at least on many days—of what I do. But when I reflect on why all this is true, one thing is clear: It's *not* because I had a clear sense of direction at the outset!

I've learned a great deal about high-quality teaching from things that worked in my classroom—and things that didn't—and from watching teachers whose work speaks of excellence. Of the many elements and practices that make up the architecture of effective teaching, I offer here five that I have come to believe are foundational.

Find a Place That Fits You

Teaching is hard. Teachers at every stage need to be cultivated. That's certainly the case in the novice years, when a teacher is practicing who he or she will become. It's important for each fledgling teacher to find an environment that nurtures fearless practice and discovery. Early in my journey as an accidental teacher, I taught in three settings for roughly a year each. In each place, I learned an immense amount, and each place contributed significantly to my understanding of teaching. Two of the schools had relatively toxic environments; the third was neutral. I'm not sorry I worked in any of these settings, but I would have been a very different teacher—and not as good a one—had I remained in any of them for long.

The fourth school in which I taught was precisely the right setting for me during the years I was there. It was relatively small; in a larger place, I would have been lost. It was, when I began teaching there, fairly unsophisticated in its pedagogy and expectations. That, too, was right for me; I'd have felt like a failure in a cutting-edge place. The community was embracing; and I needed the sense of being known, welcomed, and trusted. The district leadership was, for the most part, open to new ideas. In that way, the school was an incubator for creative teaching.

During the years I worked at this school, the community, the district, and the school changed in a way that mirrored my own development. We grew up together, which continued to make the place fresh and challenging for me for nearly two decades. Leaving there was wrenching. I wanted more than anything to continue teaching in that place that stretched and nurtured me.

Serendipitously—accidentally?—an opportunity to be part of a university faculty opened up just at the point when the district leadership changed. I would not have accepted the university position, however—I would not even have noticed it—except that the new leadership felt pernicious to me and I sensed that remaining in the school would erode my growth rather than contribute to it.

I wasn't able to articulate all my thinking at that point, but here's what I know now: The places in which we teach shape who and what we become. If they don't feed us as human beings and as teachers, we atrophy. In teaching and in life, if we are not growing, we are losing ground. So a school, school district, and community need to be the right fit at the right time to fuel our professional and personal evolution.

Understand Teaching as a Calling

A job is something that has to be done to receive a paycheck. All legitimate jobs are worthy, of course, but a calling is something more. It challenges us to be more than we think we can be and to draw on capacities we didn't quite know we had. A calling becomes a way of life, offering us the opportunity to affect individuals in a profound, enduring way.

I once asked two nurses in difficult hospital settings why they each did what they did. The first said, "because I am most fully alive when I'm here." The second responded, "because I can give people hope when they are in pain and companionship when that's all that's left." I found it interesting that neither spoke about the actual medicine they were practicing or the routines they followed every day. Those things were integral to their success, yet these two people did not see their knowledge and skills as ends, but rather as tools in service of something greater. If I get sick, I hope I'll have the good fortune to be aided by someone who is knowledgeable about medicine, but who also, like these two nurses, feels called to do everything feasible to help me heal—and who feels most fully alive while doing so.

Great teachers are like those nurses. They feel called to connect content and kids. They understand that they interpret shared human wisdom, codified in the academic disciplines, to young people who need to make sense of life. They look at both the content they teach and the people whom they ask to learn that content with considerable reverence, and they find what Steven Levy (1996) calls the genius in both content and in students. They dignify whom and what they teach by making the act of learning dynamic and compelling.

Know You Don't Know

Excellent teachers never fall prey to the belief that they are good enough. The best teachers I have known are humbled by how much more they need to learn. They don't add to the chorus of voices chiming, "I already do that."

High-quality educators are determined and often voracious learners. They seek daily to understand their content more fully, to probe the mystery of the young lives before them more deeply, and to extend their pedagogical reach beyond yesterday's boundaries. They know that the parameters of their own lives are extended every time they extend possibilities in students' lives.

These teachers seek out the best professional development opportunities. They read about education. When a district or school fails to support their learning meaningfully, they become their own professional developers.

Two years ago, as I conducted a multiday workshop in the late spring, I became aware of one older man within the group. His questions were interesting, and it was clear he was engaged with the ideas. At a break, this man came up to ask me another question. During our conversation, he remarked wistfully that he would soon be retiring after 40 years as a classroom teacher. My first response was to ask him why he'd chosen to come to a professional development session on a complex topic so close to his retirement date.

"Oh," he replied, almost surprised by my question, "I promised myself that I would learn something new every single day I was a teacher. I've kept that promise for four decades. I'll keep it until the day I close the classroom door behind me." He paused for a moment and continued, "How else could I have been the teacher my students needed?"

Associate Yourself with Quality

The pursuit of quality occurs on at least three levels.

Develop friendships with colleagues who set high standards. Such educators are in every school, and their partnership provides both light and energy for professional growth. It's as true in the teaching life as in high school that we take on the attributes of those we hang out with. When we spend what little free time we have at school with colleagues who watch the clock or who have ready reasons to dismiss whatever threatens the status quo, we're more likely to have our aspirations lowered than raised.

I am a better teacher many times over because of people like Diane Wiegel, Judy Schlim, Debbie Kiser, Nancy Brittle, Sandra Mitchell, Mary Ann Smith, Dick Rose, and so many other colleagues who constantly reminded me of what excellence in the classroom looks like—and what is required to achieve that level of quality. Those teachers are roughly my own age. But I also learned much from Mrs. Gardner, who taught next to me during my accidental first year of teaching. It was her final year as a classroom teacher. She modeled excellence in everything she did, answered my naïve questions efficiently, listened when I was discouraged, and offered suggestions she knew were within my reach. She informally provided my first meaningful course in education over the eight months that I knew her.

As a more seasoned teacher, I learned from top-rate new guys on the block like George Murphy. Teachers like George, infused with the brash energy of youth, brought knowledge and strategies that I found fresh and renewing. For example, George taught his high school biology students to understand the scientific process in an indirect and potent way by involving them with a mock archaeological dig staged by students from the previous year, which involved hypothesizing about what was revealed by the artifacts they discovered. Then he reinforced that understanding by having them stage a dig for the next year's biology students. Through this project, students had to encounter uncertainty, look for clues, hypothesize, test conclusions, and so on.

There's something to be learned from everyone, and there's rarely a reason to be unwelcoming to anyone. Nonetheless, it makes a difference when professional friendships multiply your effectiveness rather than deplete it.

Develop a keen sense of what quality looks like. Such organizations as the National Board for Professional Teaching Standards, the National Association for the Education of Young Children, the National

Middle School Association, and the National Association of Secondary School Principals have delineated the attributes of high-quality teaching. Many books now exist that break down the elements of great teaching—Charlotte Danielson's *Enhancing Professional Practice: A Framework for Teaching* (ASCD, 2007); James Stronge's *Qualities of Effective Teachers* (ASCD, 2007); Ron Brandt's *Powerful Learning* (ASCD, 1998); or the National Research Council's *How People Learn* (National Academies Press, 2000), to name just a few. These would have been a godsend to me as a young teacher. I was largely on my own to discover the characteristics of high-quality work; my focus would have been sharper and my progress faster had I had such resources to draw on. Great teaching is both a science and an art, and many educators who are both scientists and artists can provide rubrics that point the way to excellence.

Seek quality from students. We compliment young people by asking them for their best and supporting them in achieving it. Ron Berger (2003) talks about building "an ethic of excellence in the classroom" so that students take pride in producing work that reflects their highest possible effort. Clearly this not only benefits both individual learners and society, but also benefits teachers. When we ask students to give their very best, we are obligated to be sure the work we assign is worthy of that level of effort. In learning how to explain quality to young learners, we become clearer about how it looks in our own work.

Generate Your Own Energy

It's a reality that in every human endeavor, those who are most successful work the hardest. In *Outliers*, in which Malcolm Gladwell (2008) describes boundary-breaking people in fields from technology to music, Gladwell notes that it was relentless effort more than raw talent that helped these professionals reshape their fields. We have no reason to assume otherwise in teaching.

Most teachers can mount a defense that they work hard. What makes the difference in the work ethic of high-quality teachers is that their work is regenerative; they draw energy from what they do. They achieve the state that Mihalyi Csikszentmihalyi (1990) calls *flow*, a highly satisfying condition in which an individual feels aligned with a task and the work becomes its own reward. Some educators experience flow in teaching because they find their content fascinating, some because they find it rewarding to make a difference in students' lives, some because they love the creativity involved in making instruction work for a diverse group of students, and some because of the personal growth that stems from their work. Whatever the reason, teaching generates their energy rather than depletes it.

Most excellent teachers I know have "alternative energy sources," passions outside the classroom that renew their teaching energy. Those passions not only feed their teaching, but inform it as well. One teacher explained that his love of mountain climbing revealed things about himself and about the nature of teaching that he would likely never have understood without that pursuit. Another teacher said, "I give a lot of my life to teaching, and I wouldn't have it any other way. But I am a better teacher because of the times I can leave it behind for a while and give myself fully to something else."

There is no off-the-shelf blueprint for building a highly successful teacher. Yet excellent teaching, like excellence in all human endeavors, comes in significant measure from the right fit, a higher purpose, hard work, and perseverance. The truly good news is that those things are within our reach.

References

Berger, R. (2003). *An ethic of excellence: Building a culture of craftsmanship with students.* Portsmouth, NH: Heinemann.

Csikszentmihalyi, M. (1990). *Flow: The psychology of optimal experience.* New York: HarperCollins.

Gladwell, M. (2008). *Outliers: The story of success.* New York: Little, Brown.

Levy, S. (1996). *Starting from scratch: One classroom builds its own curriculum.* Portsmouth: Heinemann.

Carol Ann Tomlinson (cat3y@virginia.edu) is William Clay Parrish Jr. Professor and Chair of Educational Leadership, Foundation, and Policy at the University of Virginia in Charlottesville.

Originally published in the December 2010/January 2011 issue of *Educational Leadership, 68*(4), pp. 22–26.

New Teachers Face Three Common Challenges

Bryan Goodwin

New teachers bring energy and enthusiasm to their classrooms, but also a specific set of needs.

A teacher's first year on the job is often difficult. According to research, student achievement tends to be significantly worse in the classrooms of first-year teachers before rising in teachers' second and third years (Rivkin, Hanushek, & Kain, 2005). The steep learning curve is hard not only on students, but also on the teachers themselves: 15 percent leave the profession and another 14 percent change schools after their first year, often as the result of feeling overwhelmed, ineffective, and unsupported (Ingersoll & Smith, 2003; Smith & Ingersoll, 2004).

Surveys and case studies offer compelling insights into the areas in which new teachers commonly struggle. By effectively addressing these areas, schools can help new teachers improve their skills more quickly, thereby keeping them in the profession and raising student achievement.

Struggling with Classroom Management

The biggest challenge that surfaces for new teachers is classroom management. A 2004 Public Agenda survey found that 85 percent of teachers believed "new teachers are particularly unprepared for dealing with behavior problems in their classrooms" (p. 3). A separate survey of 500 teachers found that teachers with three years or fewer on the job were more than twice as likely as teachers with more experience (19 percent versus 7 percent) to say that student behavior was a problem in their classrooms (Melnick & Meister, 2008).

When interviewed, many beginning teachers say their preservice programs did little to prepare them for the realities of classrooms, including dealing with unruly students. "A bigger bag of classroom management tricks would have been helpful," one first-year teacher confessed (Fry, 2007, p. 225).

New teachers universally report feeling particularly overwhelmed by the most difficult students. One Australian first-year teacher interviewed for a case study observed that having a disruptive "student in my classroom is having a significant impact on my interaction with the remainder of the class ... As a first-year teacher, I don't have the professional skills to deal with this extreme behavior" (McCormack, Gore, & Thomas, 2006, p. 104). Often, classroom management difficulties can prompt new teachers to jettison many of the research-based instructional practices they learned in college (such as cooperative learning and project-based learning) in favor of a steady diet of lectures and textbooks (Hover & Yeager, 2004).

Burdened by Curricular Freedom

Another concern that new teachers commonly raise is a lack of guidance and resources for lesson and unit planning. In a recent survey of more than 8,000 Teach for America teachers nationwide, 41 percent said their schools or districts provided them with few or no instructional resources, such as lesson plans. When classroom materials were provided, they were seldom useful; just 15 percent of the respondents reported that materials were of sufficient quality for them to freely use (Mathews, 2011).

Although such curricular freedom may be welcomed by veteran teachers, it appears to be a burden for new teachers, who have not yet developed a robust repertoire of lesson ideas or knowledge of what will work in their classrooms (Fry, 2007). Case studies have observed novice teachers struggling "just trying to come up with enough curriculum" and spending 10 to 12 hours a day juggling lesson planning; grading: and the myriad demands of paperwork, committees, and extracurricular assignments (Fry, 2007, p. 225).

It's worth noting that many schools that have successfully raised low-income students' achievement have taken a distinctly different approach. Rather than letting new teachers sink or swim with lesson planning, they provide binders full of model lesson plans and teaching resources developed by veteran teachers (Chenoweth, 2009).

Sinking in Unsupportive Environments

The sink-or-swim nature of many first-year teachers' experiences frequently surfaces as another significant challenge. New teachers often report difficult interactions with colleagues, ranging from "benign neglect" of administrators (Fry, 2007, p. 229) to lack of cooperation or even hostility from veteran teachers.

One first-year teacher, for example, said a colleague flatly refused to share his lesson plans, which was "unfortunate my first year, sinking down and getting no help" (Hover & Yaeger, 2004, p. 21). Another teacher reported that a veteran member of her department came into her classes, propped his feet up on her desk, and disrupted her teaching by throwing out historical facts. "It was so degrading," she said (Hover & Yeager, 2004, p. 20).

More than anything else, novice teachers often appear to yearn for, yet seldom receive, meaningful feedback on their teaching from experienced colleagues and administrators (Fry, 2007; McCormack, Gore, & Thomas, 2006). Regrettably, teacher mentors, ostensibly assigned to provide this support, were sometimes part of the problem, dispensing little guidance, if not bad advice (Fry, 2007). In the words of one new teacher, "Some of the teachers who are mentors shouldn't be. They're not nurturing people; they've just been here the longest, and they want [the mentor position]" (Hover & Yaeger, 2004, p. 20).

How Schools Can Scaffold Success

New teachers bring energy and enthusiasm to their classrooms, but also a specific set of needs. Whereas experienced teachers might bristle at receiving classroom management tips, model lesson plans, and constructive feedback on instruction, new teachers appear to long for such supports. School administrators should recognize that, like students, new teachers need scaffolded assistance. This support should go beyond merely assigning them a mentor, a practice that only reduces five-year attrition rates by one percentage point, from 40 to 39 percent (Smith & Ingersoll, 2004).

If, however, school administrators provide mentoring and guidance, schedule common planning periods to plan lessons with colleagues, *and* reduce new teachers' workloads by providing an aide in the classroom or fewer preparations, they can cut the attrition rate of their beginning teachers by more than half—down to 18 percent (Smith & Ingersoll, 2004). This early investment in time and resources may result in long-term gains by shortening new teachers' often-perilous journeys from novice to experienced professional.

References

Chenoweth, K. (2009). *How it's being done: Urgent lessons from unexpected schools.* Cambridge, MA: Harvard Education Press.

Fry, S. W. (2007). First-year teachers and induction support: Ups, downs, and in-betweens. *The Qualitative Report, 12*(2), 216–237.

Hover, S. D., & Yeager, E. A. (2004). Challenges facing beginning history teachers: An exploratory study. *International Journal of Social Education, 19*(1), 8–26.

Ingersoll, R. M., & Smith, T. M. (2003). The wrong solution to the teacher shortage. *Educational Leadership, 60*(8), 30–33.

Mathews, J. (2011, December 18). New teacher decries lesson plan gap [blog post]. Retrieved from *Class Struggle* at *The Washington Post* at www.washingtonpost.com/blogs/class-struggle/post/new-teacher-decries-lesson-plan-gap/2011/12/17/gIQAt0C50O_blog.html

McCormack, A., Gore, J., & Thomas, K. (2006). Early career teacher professional learning. *Asia-Pacific Journal of Teacher Education, 34*(1), 95–113.

Melnick, S., & Meister, D. (2008). A comparison of beginning and experienced teachers' concerns. *Educational Research Quarterly, 31*(3), 39–56.

Public Agenda. (2004). *Teaching interrupted: Do discipline policies in today's public schools foster the common good?* New York: Author.

Rivkin, S. G., Hanushek, E. A., & Kain, J. F. (2005). Teachers, schools, and academic achievement. *Econometrica, 73*(2), 417–458.

Smith, T. M., & Ingersoll, R. M. (2004). What are the effects of induction and mentoring on beginning teacher turnover? *American Educational Research Journal, 41*(3), 681–714.

Bryan Goodwin (bgoodwin@mcrel.org) is vice president of communications, marketing, and business development at McREL, Denver, Colorado. He is the author of *Simply Better: What Matters Most to Change the Odds for Student Success* (ASCD, 2011) and coauthor of *Balanced Leadership for Powerful Learning: Tools for Achieving Success in Your School* (ASCD, 2015).

Originally published in the May 2012 issue of *Educational Leadership, 69*(8), pp. 84–85.

Essential Skills for New Teachers

H. Jerome Freiberg

Without access to the pedagogical skills of veteran teachers, many new teachers are unprepared to face the challenges of the classroom.

New teachers are often limited in their repertoire of instructional strategies. Many teachers enter the teaching field directly from university teacher preparation programs, where they mastered minimal pedagogical knowledge or skills. Often, they are not taught how to establish the positive, organized learning environment necessary for them to teach and for students to learn. Some teachers enter the field with almost no formal teacher training, through alternative certificate programs. For example, under the 2001 "Teach for Georgia" plan, college graduates with a 2.5 or higher grade point average may be certified to teach in 30 days (Coburn, 2001).

Through trial and error, new teachers develop a repertoire of teaching strategies. This haphazard process of strategy development may take several years—by which time many struggling, unprepared new teachers have already left the classroom. In addition, most of the national curriculum standards expect teachers to create active learning environments that stimulate higher-level student thinking—yet few teachers have experienced instruction in such settings. Without high-quality preparation to ready them for the challenges of the classroom, new teachers will either teach as they have been taught, or, given current teacher attrition trends, they won't teach at all. If we are to keep quality teachers, those newest to the profession must be given the support system of pedagogical knowledge that they need to succeed in the classroom.

A Framework of Skills

Professional development for new teachers should be built on a framework of research-based instructional strategies (Freiberg & Driscoll, 2000). These skills help new teachers bridge theory and practice and create high-quality learning environments in their classrooms. The strategies fall into three categories: organizing, instructing, and assessing.

Organizing Strategies

Organizing strategies include planning, lesson design, time use (time management, time on task, and pacing, for example), advancework, and classroom management. I will focus on a few of these strategies—planning, advancework, and classroom management.

New teachers usually find organizing strategies the most difficult to master. From planning to classroom management, organizing strategies are hidden from most classroom observations. Consequently, the student teacher, intern, or new teacher who observes a master teacher's classroom in the middle of the year often misses the advancework and classroom management strategies that the master teacher used during the first few days of school to set the tone for a positive learning environment. The novice teacher observing a veteran teacher's classroom sees the outcome of effective planning—a smoothly functioning lesson—but is not privy to the veteran teacher's lesson planning processes. Organizing strategies help create the necessary conditions for learning—and teachers can acquire these skills systematically rather than depending on trial and error.

Planning. New teachers spend much more time planning instruction than their veteran counterparts do, often staying up late at night to plan the next day's lesson. Mentors can help new teachers with instructional planning—particularly unit planning, which allows the novice to see the bigger picture and plan backward from the end of the unit. During instructional planning, veteran teachers make decisions on the basis of learner, content, and context: Who are my learners? What information, ideas, and concepts do I want my students to grasp? Under what conditions will instruction occur?

Complete lesson planning comprises four components: initial, active, in-flight, and follow-up planning. During initial planning, teachers visualize the lesson—that is, they think through the lesson, anticipating their teaching and the students' responses. Active planning involves pulling together materials and resources for the lesson. Figure 5.1 illustrates the initial and active planning involved in creating a lesson.

Whereas initial and active planning occur before teachers present the lesson, in-flight planning occurs during the lesson and usually reflects changes in the day, such as a fire drill or a last-minute adjustment in the school schedule. In-flight planning also involves being able to change the lesson on the fly for more substantive reasons—when students aren't engaged in the activity, for example. Experienced teachers recognize the need for in-flight lesson corrections and can draw from a repertoire of strategies to make such modifications. During follow-up planning, teachers reflect on the lesson and write down what went well and what changes they need to make. Follow-up planning is crucial for new teachers to build an instructional repertoire for future lessons.

Advancework. It is difficult to teach those you don't know or work in an environment in which you are an outsider. Freiberg and Driscoll (2000) use the term *advancework* to describe what teachers do to get to know their students, the school, and the community in which they teach.

Many teachers live outside the communities in which they teach, particularly in urban schools. As a new teacher, I also lived outside the

Figure 5.1: The Instructional Planning Process	
Focus	This is my "gotcha" part of the lesson. I want the students to begin thinking about social studies as they walk in the door.
Objective	I ask myself what new ideas, concepts, knowledge, or skills my students will learn.
Explanation	I provide information, demonstrate, and give examples. I provide a link between prior knowledge and today's objective.
Check for Understanding	I use questioning, discussion, mini-chalkboards, yes/no cards, and simulations to check for understanding.
Guided Practice	I place a problem on the board and we work through it together. I check to see if each student understands the solution.
Individual Practice	I provide several other problems for the students to work on individually. Students work on some of the problems in groups.
Closure	I use several types of closure activities. The students will tell me one ideal skill they learned today. The students or I will summarize the lesson.

Adapted from Freiberg, H. J., & Driscoll, A. (2000). *Universal teaching strategies* (3rd ed.). Boston: Allyn and Bacon. Used with permission.

school's community—but I shopped there, had my car repaired and purchased gas near the school, had my hair cut at the local barbershop, and patronized the neighborhood bakery. I met many of my students and their parents in the community. Through involvement in the neighborhood, I became a member of the community rather than a tourist in it. Through gathering information about the school's neighborhood and climate, examining school resources and other materials, and getting to know the learners, advancework helps teachers establish a context for teaching and learning (Freiberg & Driscoll, 2000).

Classroom management. Good classroom management is nearly invisible. When classes are poorly managed, however, disorder and chaos steal time from learning and exhaust the teacher. Poor management can lead to student discipline problems, and sustained student misbehavior often inhibits teachers from using the engaging, interactive instructional approaches that foster student achievement and active learning, including cooperative grouping, learning centers, projects, experiments, and the use of manipulatives (Brophy, 1999; Cohen, 1994; Freiberg, Connell, & Lorentz, 2001).

Classroom management is more than discipline. It involves, among other things, the development of classroom rules and rational consequences for breaking them. Classroom management also can be measured by the seamless flow of papers between the students and the teacher, by the extent to which social justice triumphs over the "teacher's pet" concept, and by a teacher's ability to share control and promote student self-discipline.

Instructing Strategies

Cuban (1990) noted that the education reform of the past century has swung like a pendulum between an emphasis on teacher-centered and student-centered learning. In fact, instructional strategies exist on a continuum from most teacher-centered to most student-centered: lecture, demonstration, questioning, discussion, guided practice, independent practice, grouping, role play, simulation, and reflective inquiry (Freiberg & Driscoll, 2000). During a lecture, the teacher is the source of knowledge. By contrast, such student-focused activities as role play or reflective inquiry depend more on students as the sources of knowledge.

New teachers are most familiar with teacher-centered instructional strategies and often revert to them when under pressure. The good news is that, with time and experience, teachers can learn to use more student-centered instructional approaches. For example, teachers can begin to incorporate more student-directed approaches by following lectures with 2–3 minute student-to-student discussions about the information or issues presented during the lecture. Eventually teachers can incorporate cooperative learning structures, student research projects, and inquiry lessons that require students to seek knowledge from sources other than the textbook or the teacher.

Assessing Strategies

Effective teachers assess both student learning and their own professional learning. New teachers struggle with both types of assessment.

Student assessment. Most new teachers have a limited repertoire of assessing strategies and few prior experiences with alternative assessment.[1] Even maintaining student grades (in a gradebook or with grading software) is an unknown quantity to first-year teachers and is rarely taught in college methods courses or new teacher inservice training. Novice teachers must explore formal and informal measures of learning and practice constructing various assessments.

Most new teachers only have experience with the assessment measures that their teachers used when they were students: multiple choice, true/false, and short-answer essay tests. Assessing strategies, like instructing strategies, require a range of options to reflect students' diverse learning abilities—from rubrics that provide standards against which students can measure their work to portfolios that include pre- and post-activity student writing.

Self-assessment. Teachers rarely receive ongoing feedback about their teaching. Accurate feedback is a crucial component of instructional change, but teachers are dependent on others to supply the necessary data to answer the question, How am I doing? The typical teacher observation model, in which an administrator observes a teacher in his or her classroom a few times a year, leaves much to be desired.

Assessing oneself as a teacher is a highly inexact science. Teachers can glean information from a variety of sources, including student feedback and technology—audiotaping a class and then analyzing the lesson, for example. During a weeklong summer academy that I developed for teachers, Christina Planje, a first-year high school biology teacher, taught a simulated class and taped the lesson. After analyzing the lesson using a low-inference self-assessment measure (Freiberg, 1987; Freiberg & Driscoll, 2000), Planje determined that she needed to

- Allow more wait time for students to respond to higher-level questions
- Ask a question, leave time, and then call on a student
- Allow more student questions and feedback
- Narrow the topic
- Fully review previous concepts and tie this new lesson in with previous lessons
- Use more specific praise
- Stop saying OK and all right
- Do this self-assessment more often to examine and assess progress. (Planje, personal communication, Fall 1996)

Planje continued to audiotape her classroom and analyze the results. She gained insights into her teaching through self-assessment and credited a successful first year—and a nomination by her superintendent for a national award as the district's best first-year teacher—to her new understanding.

What can schools do to ensure new teachers' success? In addition to providing novices with mentors, schools can

- Gear "just in time" staff development to the immediate pedagogical needs of new teachers—for example, offer training that provides teaching strategies to help them get started at the beginning of the school year. Regular follow-up workshops should be scheduled as needs arise.
- Implement new teacher summer academies that provide intensive weeklong instruction in teaching and learning. Embedded in such instruction should be opportunities for

self-assessment—audiotaped lesson simulations, for example—as well as mentoring support and feedback.
- Collaborate with leaders of teacher preparation and alternative certification programs to codevelop methods courses for new teachers.
- Design an online library of veteran teachers' lesson plans that new teachers can access for ideas and instructional development.
- Establish a confidential "help line" to answer new teachers' questions.

When professors, principals, and mentor teachers expose novice educators to the framework of essential teacher skills—organizing, instructing, and assessing—new teachers can build pedagogical repertoires as rich as those of the best veteran teachers—in less time. Such training may be the crucial factor that helps more new teachers succeed and remain in the profession.

Endnote

[1] Teachers may find additional assessment resources at www.nagb.org/naep/student/background.html, www.nrrf.org/lyon_statement3-01.htm, and www.fairtest.org/princind.htm.

Author's note: This article is based on Freiberg and Driscoll, *Universal Teaching Strategies*, 3rd ed. (Allyn and Bacon, 2000).

References

Brophy, J. (1999). Perspectives of classroom management: Yesterday, today, and tomorrow. In H. J. Freiberg (Ed.), *Beyond behaviorism* (pp. 44–55). Needham Heights, MA: Allyn and Bacon.
Coburn, R. (2001). *Saving the StarFish: Recruiting and retaining qualified teachers and principals.* Atlanta, GA: Bell South.
Cohen, E. (1994). *Designing groupwork: Strategies for the heterogeneous classroom.* New York: Teachers College Press.
Cuban, L. (1990, January/February). Reforming again, again, and again. *Educational Researcher, 19*(1), 3–13.

Freiberg, H. J. (1987). Principal supervision and teacher self-assessment. *NASSP Bulletin, 71*(498), 85–92.

Freiberg, H. J., Connell, M. L., & Lorentz, J. (2001). The effects of Consistency Management on student mathematics achievement in seven Chapter I elementary schools. *Journal of Education for Students Placed At Risk, 6*(3), 249–270.

Freiberg, H. J., & Driscoll, A. (2000). *Universal teaching strategies* (3rd ed.). Boston: Allyn and Bacon.

Copyright © 2002 H. Jerome Freiberg.

H. Jerome Freiberg (freiberg@mail.uh.edu) is the John & Rebecca Moores University Professor and founder of Consistency Management & Cooperative Discipline (www.coe.uh.edu/cmcd) at the University of Houston.

Originally published in the March 2002 issue of *Educational Leadership, 59*(6): pp. 56–60.

The Challenges of Supporting New Teachers: A Conversation with Linda Darling-Hammond

Marge Scherer

In this interview with Educational Leadership, *Linda Darling-Hammond describes the kind of preparation and support new teachers need to survive their critical first years in the classroom.*

Fifty years ago, Dan Lortie said the new teacher was like Robinson Crusoe, marooned on an island and facing challenges of survival. Modern *Survivor* images aside, is it still like that for beginning teachers?

It's still like that for some teachers, but less so than it once was. It's true that a number of beginners leave the teaching profession early because they don't feel effective. Sometimes they feel that they're crashing and burning, and sometimes, they really are.

But now most states have implemented some sort of professional development or peer assistance for new teachers. About three-fourths of new teachers report that they have participated in an induction program and have had a mentor teacher assigned to them.[1] A few states even have fully funded mentoring programs in which the mentors are expert teachers who have release time to be in the classroom coaching on a regular basis.

It's really important for beginners to have systematic, intense mentoring in the first year. Having weekly support and in-classroom coaching in the first year for fine-tuning skills, for planning lessons, and for problem solving about things that come up in the classroom ensures that someone experienced is there during the critical moments of the beginning teacher's first year.

That is the ideal way to make sure beginning teachers don't just survive but also become competent and effective—and stay in the profession.

You've noted that teacher preparation plays a big role in the retention of teachers. How does teacher preparation need to change?

In the old-style program, you took a bunch of courses and then did eight weeks of student teaching at the end of the courses. Candidates learned things in the abstract and then tended to forget much of what they learned by the time they actually got into a classroom. And the practices in their student-teaching classroom might not resemble those described in their courses. That antiquated, fragmented program is becoming a thing of the past.

Many teacher education programs have already changed so that they offer strong clinical experience connected to coursework. Many also have strengthened their preparation for curriculum development, assessment, and differentiated instruction. These things matter for keeping teachers in the profession.

We know that teachers who are fully prepared stay in teaching at much higher rates than those who lack key elements of preparation. Those who have done student teaching are less than half as likely to leave after the first year as those who haven't student taught. Those who have had coaching, been observed in their classrooms, and seen other people teach are less than half as likely to leave within the first year. Those who have had a chance to study child development, learning, and curriculum are less than half as likely to leave as those who have not had those opportunities.[2]

Being in the classroom of an effective mentor teacher for a long enough period of time, with graduated responsibilities, has a huge impact. Carefully managed student-teaching placement matters, too.

What is the current status of the professional development school? Has that movement been successful?

I just gave a talk to about 1,000 people at the annual conference of the National Association of Professional Development Schools. They came from across the United States and from several other nations and were all involved with thriving professional development schools. Many universities and schools together provide not only a clinical site for training teachers in the context of carefully mentored student teaching, but also a coherent program in which all of the courses are connected to the clinical work.

In these programs, the student learns specific practices, goes into the classroom and works on those practices, and then brings the experience back (sometimes with a videotape of the teaching or evidence of student work), debriefs, problem solves, learns some more, and takes it back to use in the classroom.

Of course, this requires collaborative planning between faculties in both the school and the university. The most powerful program models now enroll students in student teaching from the time they enter through the time they complete the program. Courses and student teaching are woven around each other, like a double helix.

Would you name a few of the professional development schools that have model programs?

I can name well over 100 schools that are doing very fine work.

It's certainly the model we use at Stanford. You see very high-quality work going on at Bank Street College, Columbia University, the University of Connecticut, the University of New Hampshire, the University of Michigan, Michigan State University, the University of South Carolina, and Trinity University in San Antonio, Texas, among many others.

Why aren't we hearing about such programs more often?

In the United States right now, there is a tendency to assert that teacher education doesn't matter and that we don't have any good teacher education programs. There are some very weak programs still, and that's a problem we need to solve by raising the floor with stronger accreditation.

Because we don't talk much about the really good programs, these models don't drive improvement in the field as much as they could.

The alternative, short-term teacher prep programs are now training many new teachers. How have these programs affected the profession as a whole?

The initial rationale for alternative routes into teaching was a useful one: to provide options for older candidates who had already completed college. Twenty years ago, most teacher education was undergraduate only. Alternatives were designed, first and foremost, to provide pathways into teaching for people who already had a bachelor's degree. Many were graduate-level programs, awarding a Master of Arts in Teaching and lasting 12–18 months. They integrated intensive preservice clinical work and coursework in a thoughtful way. Some others provided coursework on a more flexible part-time basis so that candidates could begin preparation while they were employed at other jobs (for example, in transition from military employment).

Another good thing about many alternative routes was that they provided pathways directly into the districts that needed to hire the teachers—both urban and rural districts—where the shortages were.

The challenge we have with alternative programs now is that they are all over the map. Some offer high-quality programs and include enough coursework and student teaching to ensure that candidates are truly ready to teach. The graduates are well prepared, and they are well supported once they get in the classroom.

But there are also a lot of alternatives that offer only a few weeks of training in the summer before a teacher is thrown in as the teacher of record in the fall, without enough background knowledge or practice teaching. Then the promised mentoring support often does not materialize adequately. A lot of people coming in through those routes are not well prepared to teach. They struggle and flounder, and it hurts their students. Such routes also have very high attrition rates from teaching, leaving a lot of churn in their wake.

The core value of every profession is that everyone in the profession has a common body of knowledge and skills needed to be responsible and effective. When you have a lot of people coming in with very little training, confidence in the profession goes down. Lowering standards also drives salaries down, which then makes it hard to recruit and keep good people in the profession. The whole enterprise of teaching is seriously undermined.

When some people can't be trusted to know what to do, the system tends to respond by trying to micromanage teaching for everyone, mandating pacing guides and scripted texts. Lee Shulman used to call it an effort to create remote control of teaching.

The problem with standardizing teaching in that way is that *children* are not standardized. They don't learn in the same way or at the same pace. And if you are really engaged in professional teaching, you are trying to meet the needs of individual children. These responses to lack of confidence in teachers end up undermining instruction for children.

What policy change would be effective in attracting the best and brightest to the teaching profession?

The current conventional wisdom that teachers are not academically able is often wrong. A so-called "fact" that I often hear repeated is that most U.S. teachers are recruited from the bottom third of the class. That has not been true since the mid-1980s.

In fact, the most recent large-scale study on this question comes from Educational Testing Service, which tracked the SATs for teachers who completed preparation and sat for licensing examinations through 2005.[3] From 1994 to 2005, there was a strong improvement in academic ability of entrants to the profession. By 2005, the average entering high school teacher scored well above the average college student in SAT verbal scores, and entering math and science teachers far outscored other college students in SAT math scores. Entering elementary teachers scored just above 500 on the SAT verbal and math tests. Over 80 percent of entering teachers had a college grade point average of 3.0 or above. So the bar has been raised, and we have been getting, nationwide, an increasingly high caliber of prospective teachers.

What are the reasons for the change?

There are much higher standards now than there were in the 1980s. Most states require a basic skills test, and many require a minimum grade point average to enter teacher training. Most require a test of subject-matter knowledge either before or after training. Some states have other licensure tests on top of those.

Because of No Child Left Behind (NCLB) requirements and changes in state policy, today most secondary teachers receive a major in a content area, as do many elementary teachers. Fewer than half of those entering teaching receive an education major, and the expectations for education majors and minors have increased substantially in most states and universities.

In states with high standards—for example, Massachusetts, Connecticut, and New York—many high-ability people are coming into teaching. Even in states with lower standards—for example, Texas and Florida—individual universities often have higher standards than their states require. At top universities in the United States—like Columbia, Stanford, the University of California, and the University of

Connecticut—the people who come into teacher education programs typically have SAT and GRE scores above the 80th or 90th percentile. They're every bit as academically able, and sometimes even more so, than the people in their doctoral programs.

Do we really need the best and the brightest to enter the profession?

We certainly want intelligent, academically capable people coming into teaching. Do they need to have 99th percentile SAT scores? That score, by itself, is not predictive of the capacity to teach. Some very smart people do not make good teachers. They don't have the interpersonal skills. They don't have the capacity to manage 55 things at once as teachers must do in a classroom.

We want in teachers a combination of strong academic ability and the capacities to be very alert and attentive, to care about kids, to be able to understand what kids are doing and what they mean by it, and to manage classrooms and support children. And, to be a good teacher, you have to care more about the performance of your students and how they learn than about your own performance.

Some very academically able people who go into teaching are used to getting rewarded for things they do by themselves. But it's a very different thing to help other people succeed. In teaching, your effectiveness doesn't depend on your own efforts alone. It depends on how well you can support and motivate your students to work at learning.

What can we learn from other countries about attracting the right kind of teachers?

There are several things to learn. If you look at the countries that once were not high achieving, but now are both high achieving and equitable in their student outcomes, you'll see that they have invested in teacher preparation and development programs to accomplish those gains. Finland, Singapore, and South Korea, for example, not only invest in high-quality preparation, but also pay all of the costs for candidates to get that preparation. They also give candidates a stipend while they are in training, so that no one has to go into debt to enter teaching or suffer from less preparation than they need.

So we could easily recruit and retain the best and brightest teachers if we actually made good on what President Obama said when he was campaigning: "If you will teach, we'll pay for your college education."

States that have done that have raised the bar. For many years, the North Carolina Teaching Fellows underwrote top high school students' college education at state universities where they prepared to teach and added additional summer coursework to help them learn to become education leaders. In exchange for this support, candidates pledged to teach for at least four years in North Carolina schools. The state brought many thousands of high-ability people into teaching that way, with a disproportionate number of them in high-need fields like math and science, plus a large representation of men and minority candidates, who are usually in short supply. A follow-up study seven years later showed that more than 75 percent of these folks were still in teaching, and some of the remainder were already working in education administration.

North Carolina Teaching Fellows did essentially what some nations have done: select and support high-ability people who have demonstrated a commitment and enthusiasm to work with children. These people not only enter but also build their careers in the profession and become leaders and raise up the whole system.

And why isn't this happening more often?

There is unfortunately a lot of teacher bashing and bad-mouthing of the profession these days. Some politicians and philanthropists have adopted a very punitive and shortsighted approach—putting an emphasis on sanctions based on test scores and not on training, development, or equalization of resources, and then urging the firing of teachers whose students do not score well on tests. This leaves teachers underprepared and undersupported to do the important job they need to do. It is no way to build a profession. In fact, it creates an anti-profession.

I just read the MetLife Survey of the American Teacher, which said that U.S. teachers' satisfaction with their profession had declined 15 points. Is that surprising to you?

I just looked at that, too, and it's not surprising. That drop in satisfaction was in just two years after 2009. The decline was closer to 20 percentage points if you go back to 2008. The survey also showed that the proportion of teachers planning to leave had increased by 12 percent in just two years. These last three years have been devastating for teaching. All over the United States I hear from teachers that they are discouraged, particularly by the way national discourse assumes that all the ills of the system are the sole fault of teachers.

And it's going to become much, much worse as test-based teacher evaluation is rolled out. Researchers have extensive evidence that the ratings teachers get from these value-added systems are hugely error-prone, unreliable, and to a great extent, shaped by which students are assigned to a teacher in a given year.[4]

All of the things that are happening to undermine education today—larger class sizes, fewer days in the school year, reductions in the number of reading specialists and tutors, growing poverty and homelessness among children—influence achievement gains and contribute to what is being called a "teacher effectiveness" rating. The effect of everything that matters for learning is being attributed to the teacher alone. And teachers who teach the highest-need students are most affected by both the unfairness of current education policies and the bias in teacher effectiveness ratings.

What are better ways to evaluate teachers, especially beginning teachers?

We know a lot now about how to undertake high-quality performance assessments of teachers. Since the National Board for Professional Teaching Standards portfolio was created in the late 1980s, several states have developed similar assessments for beginning teachers.

Teachers are asked to plan a unit of instruction linked to the standards in their content area, to adapt their plans for English learners and students with special needs, to teach the unit, and then to be videotaped while teaching these lessons. They also collect evidence of student learning and analyze both their teaching and the student learning that resulted.

Connecticut developed its BEST Portfolio to guide learning for beginning teachers and then to determine the candidates' readiness for a professional credential after two years in the classroom. Research shows that the scores on that portfolio significantly predicted teachers' effectiveness with students.

There are now 27 states piloting a national version of a performance assessment for the initial license, which builds on the success of California's Performance Assessment for Teachers. A number of those states are beginning to think about also using a related performance assessment during the first two or three years of teaching that continues to build on the initial portfolio and that could become the basis for achieving the professional credential. These kinds of tools, plus the kinds of close-in evaluation and support provided by mentors in districts that have adopted peer assistance and review programs, have also been found to improve effectiveness.

That's what we should be doing with beginning teachers: using professional teaching standards and thoughtful support and evaluation processes to give them the feedback that they need.

One last point on the test-based teacher evaluations: Teachers who are subjected to those systems are saying that they can't draw any relationship between what they do from year to year and how their ratings bounce around. As a teacher in Houston put it: "I do what I do every year. I teach the way I teach every year. My first year got me pats on the back. My second year got me kicked in the backside. And for year three my scores were off the charts. I got a huge bonus, and now I am in the top quartile of all the English teachers. What did I do differently? I have no clue."[5]

So a test-based evaluation doesn't actually help people get better at their teaching because it's an unpredictable, erratic, confusing measure that basically puts more noise in the system.

Schools and education leaders can't always change the policies affecting teachers, but what might they do to support their teachers?

Teachers want to be in environments where they are going to be successful with students, where they're getting help to do that, where they have good colleagues, where they're working as a team. Teachers, especially those just entering the profession, are generally collaboratively oriented people.

What great schools, great principals, and great school teams know is that you support teachers by structuring group collaboration for planning curriculum, by building professional learning communities, by encouraging ongoing inquiry into practice.

The schools that build those kinds of environments give teachers continuous opportunities to grow and learn, provide the tools they need to do their job, and enable them to build good relationships with parents so they can work as partners on behalf of the child.

This may mean reorganizing the schedule, but in building those systems, leaders personalize the school environment. All of those things really are what will help teachers learn—and become happy and successful in their work.

Endnotes

[1] See Wei, R. C., Darling-Hammond, L., & Adamson, F. (2010). *Professional development in the United States: Trends and challenges*. Dallas, TX: National Staff Development Council, p. 28.

[2] Darling-Hammond, L. (2003). Keeping good teachers: Why it matters, what leaders can do. *Educational Leadership, 60*(8), pp. 6–13.

[3] Gitomer, D. (2007). *Teacher quality in a changing policy landscape: Improvements in the teacher pool*. Princeton, NJ: Educational Testing Service.

[4] Darling-Hammond, L., Amrein-Beardsley, A., Haertel, E., & Rothstein, J. (2012). Evaluating teacher evaluation. *Phi Delta Kappan, 93*(6), p. 11.

[5] Darling-Hammond, L., Amrein-Beardsley, A., Haertel, E., & Rothstein, J. (2012). Evaluating teacher evaluation. *Phi Delta Kappan, 93*(6), p. 11.

Linda Darling-Hammond (ldh@stanford.edu) is Charles Ducommun Professor of Education and codirector of the Stanford Center for Opportunity Policy in Education at Stanford University, California.

Marge Scherer is Editor in Chief of *Educational Leadership*.

Originally published in the May 2012 issue of *Educational Leadership, 69*(8): pp. 18–23.

Ten Roles for Teacher Leaders

Cindy Harrison and Joellen Killion

The ways teachers can lead are as varied as teachers themselves.

Teacher leaders assume a wide range of roles to support school and student success. Whether these roles are assigned formally or shared informally, they build the entire school's capacity to improve. Because teachers can lead in a variety of ways, many teachers can serve as leaders among their peers.

So what are some of the leadership options available to teachers? The following 10 roles are a sampling of the many ways teachers can contribute to their schools' success.

1. Resource Provider

Teachers help their colleagues by sharing instructional resources. These might include Web sites, instructional materials, readings, or other resources to use with students. They might also share such professional resources as articles, books, lesson or unit plans, and assessment tools.

Tinisha becomes a resource provider when she offers to help Carissa, a new staff member in her second career, set up her classroom. Tinisha gives Carissa extra copies of a number line for her students to use, signs to post on the wall that explain to students how to get help when the teacher is busy, and the grade-level language arts pacing guide.

2. Instructional Specialist

An instructional specialist helps colleagues implement effective teaching strategies. This help might include ideas for differentiating instruction or planning lessons in partnership with fellow teachers. Instructional specialists might study research-based classroom strategies (Marzano, Pickering, & Pollock, 2001); explore which instructional methodologies are appropriate for the school; and share findings with colleagues.

When his fellow science teachers share their frustration with students' poorly written lab reports, Jamal suggests that they invite several English teachers to recommend strategies for writing instruction. With two English teachers serving as instructional specialists, the science teachers examine a number of lab reports together and identify strengths and weaknesses. The English teachers share strategies they use in their classes to improve students' writing.

3. Curriculum Specialist

Understanding content standards, how various components of the curriculum link together, and how to use the curriculum in planning instruction and assessment is essential to ensuring consistent curriculum implementation throughout a school. Curriculum specialists lead teachers to agree on standards, follow the adopted curriculum, use common pacing charts, and develop shared assessments.

Tracy, the world studies team leader, works with the five language arts and five social studies teachers in her school. Using standards in English and social studies as their guides, the team members agree to increase the consistency in their classroom curriculums and administer common assessments. Tracy suggests that the team develop a common understanding of the standards and agrees to facilitate the development and analysis of common quarterly assessments.

4. Classroom Supporter

Classroom supporters work inside classrooms to help teachers implement new ideas, often by demonstrating a lesson, coteaching, or observing and giving feedback. Blase and Blase (2006) found that consultation with peers

> enhanced teachers' self-efficacy (teachers' belief in their own abilities and capacity to successfully solve teaching and learning problems) as they reflected on practice and grew together, and it also encouraged a bias for action (improvement through collaboration) on the part of teachers. (p. 22)

Marcia asks Yolanda for classroom support in implementing nonlinguistic representation strategies, such as graphic organizers, manipulatives, and kinesthetic activities (Marzano et al., 2001). Yolanda agrees to plan and teach a lesson with Marcia that integrates several relevant strategies. They ask the principal for two half-days of professional release time, one for learning more about the strategy and planning a lesson together, and the other for coteaching the lesson to Marcia's students and discussing it afterward.

5. Learning Facilitator

Facilitating professional learning opportunities among staff members is another role for teacher leaders. When teachers learn with and from one another, they can focus on what most directly improves student learning. Their professional learning becomes more relevant, focused on teachers' classroom work, and aligned to fill gaps in student learning. Such communities of learning can break the norms of isolation present in many schools.

Frank facilitates the school's professional development committee and serves as the committee's language arts representative. Together, teachers plan the year's professional development program using a backmapping model (Killion, 2001). This model begins with identifying student learning needs, teachers' current level of knowledge and skills in the target areas, and types of learning opportunities that different groups of teachers need. The committee can then develop and implement a professional development plan on the basis of their findings.

6. Mentor

Serving as a mentor for novice teachers is a common role for teacher leaders. Mentors serve as role models; acclimate new teachers to a new school; and advise new teachers about instruction, curriculum, procedure, practices, and politics. Being a mentor takes a great deal of time and expertise and makes a significant contribution to the development of a new professional.

Ming is a successful teacher in her own 1st grade classroom, but she has not assumed a leadership role in the school. The principal asks her to mentor her new teammate, a brand-new teacher and a recent immigrant from the Philippines. Ming prepares by participating in the district's three-day training on mentoring. Her role as a mentor will not only include helping her teammate negotiate the district, school, and classroom, but will also include acclimating her colleague to the community. Ming feels proud as she watches her teammate develop into an accomplished teacher.

7. School Leader

Being a school leader means serving on a committee, such as a school improvement team; acting as a grade-level or department chair; supporting school initiatives; or representing the school on community or district task forces or committees. A school leader shares the vision of the school, aligns his or her professional goals with those of the school and district, and shares responsibility for the success of the school as a whole.

Joshua, staff sponsor of the student council, offers to help the principal engage students in the school improvement planning process. The school improvement team plans to revise its nearly 10-year-old vision and wants to ensure that students' voices are included in the process. Joshua arranges a daylong meeting for 10 staff members and 10 students who represent various views of the school experience, from nonattenders to grade-level presidents. Joshua works with the school improvement team facilitator to ensure that the activities planned for the meeting are appropriate for students so that students will actively participate.

8. Data Coach

Although teachers have access to a great deal of data, they do not often use that data to drive classroom instruction. Teacher leaders can lead conversations that engage their peers in analyzing and using this information to strengthen instruction.

Carol, the 10th grade language arts team leader, facilitates a team of her colleagues as they look at the results of the most recent writing sample, a teacher-designed assessment given to all incoming 10th grade students. Carol guides teachers as they discuss strengths and weaknesses of students' writing performance as a group, as individuals, by classrooms, and in disaggregated clusters by race, gender, and previous school. They then plan instruction on the basis of this data.

9. Catalyst for Change

Teacher leaders can also be catalysts for change, visionaries who are "never content with the status quo but rather always looking for a better way" (Larner, 2004, p. 32). Teachers who take on the catalyst role feel secure in their own work and have a strong commitment to continual improvement. They pose questions to generate analysis of student learning.

In a faculty meeting, Larry expresses a concern that teachers may be treating some students differently from others. Students who come to him for extra assistance have shared their perspectives, and Larry wants teachers to know what students are saying. As his colleagues discuss reasons for low student achievement, Larry challenges them to explore data about the relationship between race and discipline referrals in the school. When teachers begin to point fingers at students, he encourages them to examine how they can change their instructional practices to improve student engagement and achievement.

10. Learner

Among the most important roles teacher leaders assume is that of learner. Learners model continual improvement, demonstrate lifelong learning, and use what they learn to help all students achieve.

Manuela, the school's new bilingual teacher, is a voracious learner. At every team or faculty meeting, she identifies something new that she is trying in her classroom. Her willingness to explore new strategies is infectious. Other teachers, encouraged by her willingness to discuss what works and what doesn't, begin to talk about their teaching and how it influences student learning. Faculty and team meetings become a forum in which teachers learn from one another. Manuela's commitment to and willingness to talk about learning break down barriers of isolation that existed among teachers.

Roles for All

Teachers exhibit leadership in multiple, sometimes overlapping, ways. Some leadership roles are formal with designated responsibilities.

Other more informal roles emerge as teachers interact with their peers. The variety of roles ensures that teachers can find ways to lead that fit their talents and interests. Regardless of the roles they assume, teacher leaders shape the culture of their schools, improve student learning, and influence practice among their peers.

Authors' note: The 10 roles are described in more detail in *Taking the Lead: New Roles for Teachers and School-Based Coaches* by J. Killion and C. Harrison, 2006, Oxford, OH: National Staff Development Council. Although the names have been changed, all examples are based on actual teachers we encountered in our research.

References

Blase, J., & Blase, J. (2006). *Teachers bringing out the best in teachers: A guide to peer consultation for administrators and teachers.* Thousand Oaks, CA: Corwin Press.

Killion, J. (2001). *What works in elementary schools: Results-based staff development.* Oxford, OH: National Staff Development Council.

Larner, M. (2004). *Pathways: Charting a course for professional learning.* Portsmouth, NH: Heinemann.

Marzano, R., Pickering, D., & Pollock, J. (2001). *Classroom instruction that works.* Alexandria, VA: ASCD.

Cindy Harrison (crh@instructimprove.org) is an independent consultant at Instructional Improvement Group. **Joellen Killion** (Joellen.Killion@nsdc.org) is the Deputy Executive Director at National Staff Development Council.

Originally published in the September 2007 issue of *Educational Leadership,* 65(1): pp. 74–77.

Why Teachers Must Become Change Agents

Michael G. Fullan

Teacher education programs must help teaching candidates to link the moral purpose that influences them with the tools that will prepare them to engage in productive change.

Teaching at its core is a moral profession. Scratch a good teacher and you will find a moral purpose. At the Faculty of Education, University of Toronto, we recently examined why people enter the teaching profession (Stiegelbauer 1992). In a random sample of 20 percent of 1,100 student teachers, the most frequently mentioned theme was "to make a difference in the lives of students." Of course, such statements cannot be taken at face value because people have a variety of motives for becoming teachers. Nonetheless, there is a strong kernel of truth to this conclusion.

What happens in teacher preparation, the early years of teaching, and throughout the career, however, is another story. Those with a clear sense of moral purpose often become disheartened, and those with a limited sense of purpose are never called upon to demonstrate their commitment. In an extensive study of teacher burnout, Farber (1991) identifies the devastating effects of the growing "sense of inconsequentiality" that often accompanies the teacher's career. Many teachers, says Farber, begin their careers "with a sense that their work is socially meaningful and will yield great personal satisfactions." This sense dissipates, however, as "the inevitable difficulties of teaching . . . interact with personal issues and vulnerabilities, as well as social pressure and values, to engender a sense of frustration and force a reassessment of the possibilities of the job and the investment one wants to make in it" (1991, p. 36).

A Natural Alliance

Certainly calls for reestablishing the moral foundation of teaching are warranted, but increased commitment at the one-to-one and classroom levels alone is a recipe for moral martyrdom. To have any chance of making teaching a noble and effective profession—and this is my theme here—teachers must combine the mantle of moral purpose with the skills of change agentry.

Moral purpose and change agentry, at first glance, appear to be strange bedfellows. On closer examination they are natural allies (Fullan 1993). Stated more directly, moral purpose—or making a difference—concerns bringing about improvements. It is, in other words, a *change theme*. In addition to the need to make moral purpose more explicit, educators need the tools to engage in change productively. Moral purpose keeps teachers close to the needs of children and youth; change agentry causes them to develop better strategies for accomplishing their moral goals.

Those skilled in change appreciate its volatile character, and they explicitly seek ideas for coping with and influencing change toward some desired ends. I see four core capacities for building greater change capacity: personal vision-building, inquiry, mastery, and collaboration (see Senge 1990 and Fullan 1993). Each of these has its institutional counterpart: shared vision-building; organizational structures, norms, and practices of inquiry; the development of increased repertoires of skills and know-how among organizational members; and collaborative work cultures.

But we are facing a huge dilemma. On the one hand, schools are expected to engage in continuous renewal, and change expectations are constantly swirling around them. On the other hand, the way teachers are trained, the way schools are organized, the way the educational hierarchy operates, and the way political decision makers treat educators results in a system that is more likely to retain the status quo. One way out of this quandary is to make explicit the goals and skills of change agentry. To break the impasse, we need a new conception of teacher professionalism that integrates moral purpose and change agentry, one that works simultaneously on individual and institutional development. One cannot wait for the other.

Personal Vision-Building

Working on personal visions means examining and re-examining why we came into teaching. Asking "What difference am I trying to make personally?" is a good place to start.

For most of us, the reasons are there, but possibly buried. For the beginning teacher, they may be underdeveloped. It is time to make them front and center. Block emphasizes that "creating a vision forces us to take a stand for a preferred future" (1987, p. 102). To articulate our vision of the future "is to come out of the closet with our doubts about the organization and the way it operates" (p. 105).

Personal vision comes from within. It gives meaning to work, and it exists independently of the organization or group we happen to be in. Once it gets going, it is not as private as it sounds. Especially in moral occupations like teaching, the more one takes the risk to express personal purpose, the more kindred spirits one will find. Paradoxically, personal purpose is the route to organizational change. When it is diminished, we see in its place group-think and a continual stream of fragmented, surface changes acquired uncritically and easily discarded.

Inquiry

All four capacities of change are intimately interrelated and mutually reinforcing. The second one—inquiry—indicates that formation and enactment of personal purpose are not static matters but, rather, a perennial quest. Pascale (1990) captures this precisely: "The essential activity for keeping our paradigm current is persistent questioning. I will use the term *inquiry*. Inquiry is the engine of vitality and self-renewal" (p. 14, emphasis in original).

Inquiry is necessary for forming and reforming personal purpose. While the latter comes from within, it must be fueled by information and ideas in the environment. Inquiry means internalizing norms, habits, and techniques for continuous learning. For the beginner, learning is critical because of its formative timing. Lifelong learning is essential because in complex, ever-changing societies mental maps "cease to fit the territory" (Pascale 1990, p. 13). Teachers as change agents are career-long learners, without which they would not be able to stimulate students to be continuous learners.

Mastery

Mastery is a third crucial ingredient. People *behave* their way into new visions and ideas, not just think their way into them. Mastery is obviously necessary for effectiveness, but it is also a means for achieving deeper understanding. New mind-sets arise from mastery as much as the reverse.

It has long been known that expertise is central to successful change, so it is surprising how little attention we pay to it beyond one-shot workshops and disconnected training. Mastery involves strong initial teacher education and career-long staff development, but when we place it in the perspective of comprehensive change, it is much more than this. Beyond exposure to new ideas, we have to know where they fit, and we have to become skilled in them, not just like them.

To be effective at change, mastery is essential both in relation to specific innovations and as a personal habit.

Collaboration

There is a ceiling effect to how much we can learn if we keep to ourselves (Fullan and Hargreaves 1991). The ability to collaborate on both a small- and large-scale is becoming one of the core requisites of postmodern society. Personal strength, as long as it is open-minded (that is, inquiry-oriented), goes hand-in-hand with effective collaboration—in fact, without personal strength collaboration will be more form than content. Personal and group mastery thrive on each other in learning organizations.

In sum, the moral purpose of teaching must be reconceptualized as a change theme. Moral purpose without change agentry is martyrdom; change agentry without moral purpose is change for the sake of change. In combination, not only are they effective in getting things done, but they are good at getting the *right* things done. The implications for teacher education and for redesigning schools are profound.

Society's Missed Opportunity

Despite the rhetoric about teacher education today, there does not seem to be a real belief that investing in teacher education will yield results. With all the problems demanding immediate solution, it is easy to overlook a preventive strategy that would take several years to have an impact.

Currently, teacher education—from initial preparation throughout the career—is not geared toward continuous learning. Teacher education has the honor of being the worst problem and the best solution in education. The absence of a strong publicly stated knowledge base allows the misconception to continue that any smart person can teach. After visiting 14 colleges of education across the U.S., Kramer (1992) concludes:

> Everything [a person] needs to know about how to teach could be learned by intelligent people in a single summer of well-planned instruction (p. 24).

In a twisted way, there is some truth to this observation. It is true in the sense that many people did and still do take such minimal instruction and manage to have a career in teaching. It is true also that some people with a strong summer program would end up knowing as much or more as others who take a weak yearlong program. In her journey, Kramer found plenty of examples of moral purpose—caring people, committed to social equality. What she found wanting was an emphasis on knowledge and understanding. Caring and competence are of course not mutually exclusive (indeed this is the point), but they can seem that way when the knowledge base is so poorly formulated.

Teacher education institutions themselves must take responsibility for their current reputation as laggards rather than leaders of educational reform. I will not take up the critical area of recruitment and selection in the profession (for the best discussion, see Schlechty 1990, chapter 1). In many ways an "if you build it, they will come" strategy is called for. It is self-defeating to seek candidates who turn out to be better than the programs they enter. What is needed is a combination of selection criteria that focus on academics as well as experience (related, for example, to moral purpose), sponsorship for underrepresented groups, and a damn good program.

Teacher educators like other would-be change agents must take some initiative themselves. Examples are now happening on several fronts. At the University of Toronto, we embarked on a major reform effort in 1988. With a faculty of some 90 staff and 1,100 full-time students in a one-year post-baccalaureate teacher certification program, we piloted a number of field-based options in partnerships with school systems (see University of Toronto, *Making a Difference* Video, 1992a). In 1991 I prepared a paper for our strategic planning committee, taking as a starting point the following premise: *Faculties of Education should not advocate things for teachers or schools that they are not capable of practicing themselves*. Using a hypothetical "best faculty of education in the country" metaphor, I suggested that such a faculty would:

1. commit itself to producing teachers who are agents of educational and social improvement,
2. commit itself to continuous improvement through program innovation and evaluation,
3. value and practice exemplary teaching,
4. engage in constant inquiry,
5. model and develop lifelong learning among staff and students,
6. model and develop collaboration among staff and students,
7. be respected and engaged as a vital part of the university as a whole,
8. form partnerships with schools and other agencies,
9. be visible and valued internationally in a way that contributes locally and globally,
10. work collaboratively to build regional, national, and international networks (Fullan 1991).

To illustrate, consider items 3 and 6. It would seem self-evident that faculties of education would stand for exemplary teaching among their own staff. Faculties of education have some excellent (and poor) teachers, but I would venture to say that hardly any have effective *institutional* mechanisms for improving their own teaching. Regarding item 6, many faculties of education advocate collaborative work cultures for schools, and some participate in professional development schools. This leads to two embarrassing questions. First, to what extent are teacher preparation programs designed so that student teachers deliberately develop and practice the habits and skills of collaboration? Even more embarrassing, to what extent do university professors (arts and science, as well as education) value and practice collaboration in their own teaching and scholarship?

Key Images for Teacher Preparation

With such guiding principles, and some experience with them through our pilot projects, we at the University of Toronto have recently begun redesigning the entire teacher preparation program. Our Restructuring Committee has proposed that:

Every teacher should be knowledgeable about, committed to, and skilled in:

1. working with *all* students in an equitable, effective, and caring manner by respecting diversity in relation to ethnicity, race, gender, and special needs of each learner;
2. being active learners who continuously seek, assess, apply, and communicate knowledge as reflective practitioners throughout their careers;
3. developing and applying knowledge of curriculum, instruction, principles of learning, and evaluation needed to implement and monitor effective and evolving programs for all learners;
4. initiating, valuing, and practicing collaboration and partnerships with students, colleagues, parents, community, government, and social and business agencies;
5. appreciating and practicing the principles, ethics, and legal responsibilities of teaching as a profession;
6. developing a personal philosophy of teaching which is informed by and contributes to the organizational, community, societal, and global contexts of education (University of Toronto, B.Ed. Restructuring Committee, 1992b).

We are now developing the actual program, curriculum, and teaching designs. Everything we know about the complexities of change applies in spades to the reform of higher education institutions. Nonetheless, after four years, we have made good progress and look forward to the next four years as the ones when more comprehensive and systematic reform will be put into place (see also Goodlad 1991, Howey 1992, and the third report of the Holmes Group, forthcoming).

To summarize: Faculties of education must redesign their programs to focus directly on developing the beginner's knowledge base for effective teaching *and* the knowledge base for changing the conditions that affect teaching. Sarason puts it this way: "Is it asking too much of preparatory programs to prepare their students for a 'real world' which they must understand *and seek to change* if as persons and professionals they are to grow, not only to survive" (in press, p. 252, my emphasis). Goodlad (1991) asks a similar question: "Are a large percentage of these educators thoroughly grounded in the knowledge and skills required to bring about meaningful change?" (p. 4). The new standard for the future is that every teacher must strive to become effective at managing change.

Redesigning Schools

One of the main reasons that restructuring has failed so far is that there is no underlying conception that grounds what would happen within new structures. Restructuring has caused changes in participation, in governance, and in other formal aspects of the organization, but in the majority of cases, it has not affected the teaching-learning core and professional culture (Berends 1992, Fullan 1993). *To restructure is not to reculture.*

The professional teacher, to be effective, must become a career-long learner of more sophisticated pedagogies and technologies and be able to form and reform productive collaborations with colleagues, parents, community agencies, businesses, and others. The teacher of the future, in other words, must be equally at home in the classroom and in working with others to bring about continuous improvements.

I do not have the space to elaborate—indeed many of the details have not been worked out. The general directions, however, are clear. In terms of pedagogy, the works of Gardner (1991) and Sizer (1992)—in developing approaches to teaching for understanding—exemplify the kinds of knowledge and skills that teachers must develop and enlarge upon throughout their careers.

Beyond better pedagogy, the teacher of the future must actively improve the conditions for learning in his or her immediate environments. Put one way, teachers will never improve learning in the classroom (or whatever the direct learning environment) unless they also help improve conditions that surround the classroom. Andy Hargreaves and I developed 12 guidelines for action consistent with this new conception of "interactive professionalism":

1. locate, listen to, and articulate your inner voice;
2. practice reflection in action, on action, and about action;
3. develop a risk-taking mentality;
4. trust processes as well as people;
5. appreciate the total person in working with others;
6. commit to working with colleagues;
7. seek variety and avoid balkanization;
8. redefine your role to extend beyond the classroom;
9. balance work and life;
10. push and support principals and other administrators to develop interactive professionalism;
11. commit to continuous improvement and perpetual learning;
12. monitor and strengthen the connection between your development and students' development (Fullan and Hargreaves 1991).

We also developed eight guidelines for principals that focus their energies on reculturing the school toward greater interactive professionalism to make a difference in the educational lives of students. However, as important as principals can be, they are a diversion (and perhaps a liability) as far as new conceptions of the professional teacher are concerned. In a real sense, what gives the contemporary principalship inflated importance is the absence of leadership opportunities on the part of teachers (Fullan 1993).

A New Professionalism

Teacher professionalism is at a threshold. Moral purpose and change agentry are implicit in what good teaching and effective change are about, but as yet they are society's (and teaching's) great untapped resources for radical and continuous improvement. We need to go public with a new rationale for why teaching and teacher development are fundamental to the future of society.

Above all, we need action that links initial teacher preparation and continuous teacher development based on moral purpose and change agentry with the corresponding restructuring of universities and schools and their relationships. Systems don't change by themselves. Rather, the actions of individuals and small groups working on new conceptions intersect to produce breakthroughs (Fullan 1993). New conceptions, once mobilized, become new paradigms. The new paradigm for teacher professionalism synthesizes the forces of moral purpose and change agentry.

References

Berends, M. (1992). "A Description of Restructuring in Nationally Nominated Schools." Paper presented at the Annual Meeting of the American Educational Research Association, San Francisco.

Block, P. (1987). *The Empowered Manager*. San Francisco: Jossey-Bass.

Farber, B. (1991). *Crisis in Education*. San Francisco: Jossey-Bass.

Fullan, M. (1991). "The Best Faculty of Education in the Country: A Fable." Submitted to the Strategic Planning Committee. Faculty of Education, University of Toronto.

Fullan, M. (1993). *Change Forces: Probing the Depths of Educational Reform*. London: Falmer Press.

Fullan, M., and A. Hargreaves. (1991). *What's Worth Fighting for in Your School?* Toronto: Ontario Public School Teachers' Federation; Andover, Mass.: The Network; Buckingham, U.K.: Open University Press; Melbourne: Australian Council of Educational Administration.

Gardner, H. (1991). *The Unschooled Mind*. New York: Basic Books.

Goodlad, J. (1991). "Why We Need a Complete Redesign of Teacher Education." *Educational Leadership* 49(3), 4–10.

Holmes Group. (In press). *Tomorrow's Colleges of Education*. East Lansing, Mich.: Holmes Group.

Howey, K. R. (1992). *The Network of Fifteen*. Columbus: Ohio State University.

Kramer, R. (1992). *Ed School Follies*. New York: Foss Press.

Pascale, P. (1990). *Managing on the Edge*. New York: Touchstone.

Sarason, S. (In press). *The Case for a Change: The Preparation of Educators*. San Francisco: Jossey-Bass.

Schlechty, P. (1990). *Reform in Teacher Education*. Washington, D.C.: American Association of Colleges of Education.

Senge, P. (1990). *The Fifth Discipline*. New York: Doubleday.

Sizer, T. (1992). *Horace's School: Redesigning the American High School*. Boston: Houghton Mifflin.

Stiegelbauer, S. (1992). "Why We Want to Be Teachers." Paper presented at the Annual Meeting of the American Educational Research Association, San Francisco.

University of Toronto, Faculty of Education. (1992a). *Making a Difference* Video, Toronto, Ontario.

University of Toronto, Faculty of Education. (1992b). "B.Ed. Restructuring Committee Report," Toronto, Ontario.

Michael G. Fullan is Dean of Education at the University of Toronto.

Originally published in the March 1993 issue of *Educational Leadership*, 50(6): pp. 12–17.

The Problem-Solving Power of Teachers

Ariel Sacks

The best solutions to problems in education may just come from those closest to students.

I entered teaching about 10 years ago, eager to change the way the school experience was constructed for young people. At that time, I could hardly have imagined the constant spin of changes that would take hold of schools and my chosen profession. Now the U.S. public education system seems to have become a veritable smorgasbord of education experiments.

Risk takers of all kinds have joined the effort to find new and better ways to structure nearly every aspect of teaching and learning. Some of the experiments I'm seeing in schools are positive—more teacher teams, for example—and others trouble me—like giving strong teachers dramatically larger classes.

I know we need to be willing to try new things to find out what does and doesn't work. But sadly, most of the experiments in education reform come from the imaginations of people who don't actually teach children. The Common Core State Standards Initiative may be the biggest and most obvious current example of this. A team of 50 writers that included just one teacher designed what has been called "the most far-reaching experiment in American educational history" (Hacker & Dreifus, 2013).[1] It's hard not to feel the implicit message when such a huge endeavor was decided on with only token teacher input.

All feelings aside, top-down experiments often end up being out of sync with the realities of both teachers and students. As teachers well know, the details matter; a great idea on paper can easily be rolled out ineffectively. Although teachers understand the value of learning from mistakes, we've seen so many mistakes lately that it's hard not to conclude that it's time to start taking risks on teachers and their problem-solving abilities. Let us solve some of the problems that have such an effect on our classrooms! It's what we do every day; we just work from a limited domain.

Let me illustrate the problem-solving power of teachers by recounting a story from my school in which a grade-level team of teachers turned a small-scale dysfunctional policy into a system that improved both struggling students' academic performance and teacher efficacy.

A Harmless Policy in Theory . . .

For the last few years, my school has had what seemed like a reasonable policy about missing homework: If a student missed two homework assignments in a single week, the student was required to serve an after-school detention. The dean of students organized and maintained detention sessions, which were held on Wednesday afternoons. (This was fitting, because Wednesday was our school's official "no homework" day.) The teacher simply needed to notify the parent of the date of the detention, receive confirmation, and place the student's name on a list.

Sounds clear and easy, right? In theory.

As a teacher, I remember thinking, OK, I'll probably need to put in a lot of work at the beginning of the year assigning detention to all the students who don't turn in homework, but the investment will be worth it when the students develop the habit of doing their homework on time. Not having to hold detention in my own classroom seemed like a good perk.

But a Messy Policy in Practice

In practice, teachers ended up spending hours on Friday afternoons e-mailing or calling the families of the numerous students who had missed two or more homework assignments that week. Phone conversations could get lengthy, so a generic e-mail template seemed like a better bet.

Even then, the hours started to add up when we began to receive reply messages from parents. These included questions about the specifics of the assignments, claims that parents saw their child working on the assignment and requests that the student be able to turn it in the following day, interest from parents in overseeing their child doing the assignment at home, requests from parents to contact them whenever their child did not turn in homework, and requests to reschedule the detention because of scheduling conflicts. It wasn't that we didn't want to have conversations with parents about their child's work in class. It's just that assigning detention didn't create a positive entry point into such a conversation.

The process was overwhelming, and correspondences easily dragged from Friday, across the weekend, all the way through the Wednesday of the actual detention. Moreover, because teachers weren't present during detention periods, there was no guarantee that students would even work on the assignments they'd missed. And if a student had avoided homework because he or she didn't understand the assignment, detention wasn't structured to offer that help.

The result of the clunky policy was that some teachers continued to put in an inordinate amount of time assigning homework detention, and others just took matters into their own hands, circumventing the system.

In my class, for example, the homework is typically to read, and students must keep up with a pacing calendar. By the time students served detention, however, they were often even more behind schedule, and one hour of detention wasn't going to be enough for them to catch up. What I needed was support from parents in ensuring that students read outside class.

I started to simply contact the parents of students who were more than a day or two behind the pacing calendar. I would do this by e-mail or in a phone call on my way home. This communication with parents seemed more effective than calling them about detention, because it began a dialogue; it made parents my allies, rather than putting them on the spot.

Inconsistent and Confusing

When teachers took matters into their own hands, students began to receive mixed messages across classes about consequences. School leaders couldn't get an accurate idea of any individual student's homework completion rate or track the habits of the larger group. They couldn't be sure that teachers were contacting parents or following up on students who missed assignments. Most teachers, myself included, had weeks during which we failed to follow up on missing homework altogether (because of exhaustion or other demands on our time). Meanwhile, some of these students were falling through the cracks, and parents were often under the impression that everything was fine.

From the teachers' side, it was frustrating, because typically the same students failed to submit homework over and over again—and these same students often didn't complete class work or projects either. The problem was deeper than homework detentions could fix.

Teachers Devise a Solution

Teachers at my school meet twice each month in grade-level teams. During this time, we coordinate our advisory program, discuss student progress, and strategize in response to student needs. In addition to teaching 8th grade English language arts, I lead my grade-level team. The homework detention issue had come up in the past, but we hadn't been able to envision a solution that seemed worthy of proposing to our principal—until recently.

This year, an improved schoolwide schedule provides us with time at the end of the official school day, which we didn't have in the past. We teachers now offer daily "office hours" in our classrooms for students looking for extra help on assignments. In a team meeting a few months ago, we were discussing the issue that the students who took advantage of office hours were not always the ones we thought needed the most help.

In response, we all started encouraging those students who routinely were not completing assignments to attend office hours. We also began talking to their parents, who supported the idea. A new microproblem arose when we all encouraged the same students to attend our individual office hours on the same day—we were asking the students to be in several places at once.

That's when it hit us. "Why don't we hold 8th grade office hours in one place, and teachers can go to that location to work with students?" one teacher suggested. The wheels began to turn.

"Could we assign certain students to be in office hours every day, until further notice?" another teacher added.

"We could stop assigning homework detention for 8th graders, and just make mandatory office hours for the students who need it," someone else said. "Anyone could come to that location for office hours, but it would be mandatory for some."

We made a list of all the students who regularly missed assignments in more than one class. Most of these students also had failing grades in more than one class. The list came to around 12 students out of the 107 8th graders. Our reading teacher volunteered her room, which was large and had nice beanbag chairs and a rug. We planned to have advisors contact the parents of their advisees who were on the list and arrange for the students to attend mandatory office hours daily (except

Thursdays, when teachers have meetings) for six weeks. We would then check in on each student's progress and determine next steps.

Principal Support

I brought our plan to our principal, who supported our effort and helped me think through how to communicate the changes to those outside our team. As with any change, it took some troubleshooting to develop a fully functional system. We had to create a rotation of teachers who would be there each day, always having at least two 8th grade teachers present. More teachers would probably stop by to check in with students, but at least two would stay the whole hour. We had to create a system for taking attendance and following up. The deans lent support in the cases of students who skipped mandatory office hours.

Real-Time Results

At first, students pushed back on our expectations, wanting to use the time to play around. Fairly quickly, however, they began to break old habits and use the time to finish their work and get help from their teachers. It became a positive space, where students helped one another as much as we helped them. There were still a few students who were assigned to attend but usually didn't. But the new system allowed us to isolate these cases and focus on getting to the root of the problem.

A few months later, we could really see the positive effect of this system on our students' grades—almost all the students who attended office hours passed their classes. More students joined the group, and a few changed their homework habits so much that we allowed them to stop attending. The 7th grade team also adopted our system.

Teachers no longer spend hours chasing after students and their families over homework detention—or feeling guilty for not doing so. More students get the help they need, even if that help is nothing more than a time and place to do their homework.

Two Lessons About Teacher-Driven Reform

The first lesson we can learn from this experience is that a teacher-driven solution is often far better suited to a problem than a top-down one. Nothing was inherently wrong with the original homework detention policy; it just didn't work very well. It was difficult to see this from the outside, though. Teachers were the ones implementing the system, and we were the only ones who could see both our students and the problem clearly enough to imagine a solution. We took responsibility for fixing the problem because doing so helped us do our jobs better. There are many problems that teachers are the most capable professionals to solve.

The second lesson is about school leadership. We were able to create a better system because we had the time, autonomy, and support to do so. My school's administrators trust teachers to use our meeting time to serve our students, and they don't micromanage us with top-down agendas.

Everyone benefits when teachers have space for collaborative problem solving. The new "office hours" policy wasn't my idea, although I contributed to the conversation. Rather, I like to think it arose from the conditions that my school and I have created so that members of the team feel comfortable sharing ideas and are confident they'll be heard. If we had believed that our principal would shoot the idea down, it's doubtful we would have spent time devising the structure. But previous experience told us we had this kind of autonomy and opportunity, and it turned out we were right. My principal took a risk on our idea and supported us in putting it into practice.

A Broader Domain for Problem Solving

Teams of teachers across the United States are coming up with great ideas to improve their schools—and even more teachers could do so. So far, though, the problems that education leaders tend to trust practicing teachers to solve don't extend much beyond the realm of homework detention and other small-scale, school-based initiatives. Too many areas of education—from assessment of student learning to teacher compensation to teacher preparation—have yet to truly benefit from teachers' ideas. Instead, they often suffer from the same mismatch we saw in the seemingly sound homework detention policy.

Although leadership opportunities for teachers seem to abound, we're often relegated to being a mouthpiece for someone else's ideas or a token teacher in a plan that really doesn't use our input. I wrote about this in an article that appeared not long ago in *Education Week* (Sacks, 2012); it got so much response from educators that it was clear I'd struck a chord.

What would it take to get practicing teachers to solve larger-scale problems in education? We would need time as well as a willingness on the part of education leaders to take a risk on teachers' ideas.

The Center for Teaching Quality has been incubating teachers' ideas on major policy issues for years. Teachers have tackled such issues as performance pay and teacher preparation (Center for Teaching Quality, 2007, 2013). More recently, the center is funding the work of *teacherpreneurs*—practicing teachers who have half-time release from teaching duties to solve problems both inside and outside their schools.[2]

Don't Shut Out Teacher Thinking

Even the best of teacher ideas—mine included—need to be troubleshot and assessed by teachers along the way. Consider this example. I've just written a book on a student-centered method for teaching novels that I call *whole novels*. The whole-novel method is based on a single, radical idea: Students must read an entire literary work before analyzing it formally. The book mostly addresses the ways I've found to engage diverse groups of students in this process.

If all goes well, people will love the book and be inspired to try out the ideas. If it's really successful, perhaps someone in a position of power will decide that the whole-novel approach is a good way to change how we teach literature. Then this person might call on me to help make this happen. Suddenly I'll be in a position of power; I'll have the opportunity to make decisions for a large group of teachers—but this could easily shut out teacher thinking. Even though I wholeheartedly believe this approach is best for learners, I also know it doesn't work without the critical-thinking power of the teachers using it. Packaged as a top-down directive, my idea will become "just another mandate" for teachers to withstand. The most principled teachers will take matters into their own hands and do whatever they think their students need, despite directives from above. And guess what? Then I'll become the mismatch.

If I hope to make change in classrooms beyond my own, even I need to be open to teachers' ideas every step of the way. The role of a leader in education—whether that person is a teacher at heart, a teacherpreneur, or never was a teacher—must be to inspire and give space to teachers' problem-solving ability. This is a risk worth taking in education today.

Endnotes

[1] Correction: The statement that the Common Core State Standards were designed by "a team of 50 writers that included just one teacher" is no longer accurate. It was based on a 2009 press release from the National Governors Association (NGA). According to a more recent document from the NGA, by 2010, the "work teams" had 101 members, 5 or 6 of whom were practicing teachers, and the "feedback groups" had 34 members, 2 of whom were practicing teachers.

[2] For more ideas on how teachers can be integral to the change process, see the book I coauthored with 12 other teachers, *Teaching 2030: What We Must Do for Our Public Schools—Now and In the Future* (Teachers College Press, 2011).

References

Center for Teaching Quality. (2007). *Performance-pay for teachers*. Hillsborough, NC: Author. Retrieved from www.policyarchive.org/handle/10207/bitstreams/96445.pdf

Center for Teaching Quality. (2013). *Teaching 2030: Leveraging teacher preparation 2.0*. Hillsborough, NC: Author. Retrieved from www.teachingquality.org/sites/default/files/TEACHING_2030_Leveraging_Teacher_Preparation.pdf

Hacker, A., & Dreifus, C. (2013, June 9). Who's minding the schools? *New York Times*. Retrieved from www.nytimes.com/2013/06/09/opinion/sunday/the-common-core-whos-minding-the-schools.html

Sacks, A. (2012, October 17). Beyond tokenism: Toward the next stage in teacher leadership. *Education Week*. Retrieved from www.edweek.org/tm/articles/2012/10/17/tl_sacks.html

---

Ariel Sacks (http://arielsacks.com/) teaches 8th grade English language arts in Brooklyn, New York. She is the author of *Whole Novels for the Whole Class: A Student Centered Approach* (Jossey-Bass, 2013). She writes the Center for Teaching Quality's featured blog, *On the Shoulders of Giants*.

Originally published in the October 2013 issue of *Educational Leadership*, 71(2): pp. 18–22.

Take Back Teaching Now

Nancy Flanagan

Teachers need autonomy over their own work to engage as true professionals and bring about real change.

Several years ago, I enjoyed some success as a middle school band director. I led an award-winning program that attracted nearly half the students in my school. But I was convinced I could do more. We did exciting things—there were concerts, parades, and travel—but our daily lessons seemed to be missing something important. We never looked at the cultural roots of popular music that students listened to every day. We never explored the physics of sound or the relationship of music theory to mathematics. My students weren't creating their own music either. Our modus operandi was rehearse, rehearse, perform.

I wanted to make a difference—to broaden my students' perspectives around the importance of music in global cultures and to give them tools for enjoying and participating in music making as adults. So over the span of one school year, I changed crucial elements of my practice.

One humanities lesson I designed asked my students to think about the impact of violent and misogynistic lyrics in popular music. Parent apprehension over song lyrics is a huge deal with 7th graders, most of whom believe that they're "old enough" to see or listen to anything and that it will have no effect on their character or thinking. It's a dicey classroom topic—asking middle schoolers to look at freedom of speech, cultural norms, and increasing violence in media. But the other option was to let the marketplace manipulate my students as consumers of pop music, so it seemed worth the risk.

I spoke with my principal, telling him why I thought I could do a better job as a music teacher. He was reluctant to change a popular program, and he was especially wary of an extended lesson on song lyrics—he emphatically did not want to get phone calls from parents. Mentioning that I intended to share these plans at Back to School night did not reassure him. He told me to proceed cautiously.

My students' parents, on the other hand, were enthusiastic about an occasional break from regular rehearsal routines to study popular music, and they were intrigued by a simulated case I presented that involved two fictional students, Michael and Jessica. Michael injures Jessica in a rage, after a steady diet of songs with violent lyrics. Two parents who were lawyers volunteered to read drafts of my materials and help clarify legal issues, balancing the constitutional right to publish and distribute artistic media with important reasons to guard against a violence-soaked culture. I used examples from real songs as well as faux lyrics to illustrate how easy it is to become desensitized to anger and misogyny; there were no parent objections.

The Michael and Jessica simulation was one of the most productive and satisfying pedagogical experiences in my 30-year career in the classroom. The questions that students raised varied from year to year, but they never failed to explore the role of music in shaping their own lives and cultural norms. For example, many of my students assumed that they were immune to the influence of media, but they were willing to consider that younger children might be pressured or harmed by inappropriate lyrics. We also tackled the question of free speech: Are there legal protections against potentially harmful media? Do artists have the right to make brutality seem acceptable? Eventually, the lesson materials were shared with teachers and schools around the United States.

The Michael and Jessica case was my first experiment in exploring big issues in the arts. I was soon reserving Mondays for humanities lessons, delving into composition, music history, world music, and links among music and other artistic modes. I stopped thinking in terms of the next performance and began teaching and assessing a broader range of musical knowledge.

How was I able to make such changes in curriculum, instruction, and assessment—including tackling tricky subjects? I was a veteran teacher, well-known and trusted in the community. I was teaching a subject that was not tested; students elected to be in my class. I didn't act alone—I shared nontraditional ideas and goals with colleagues and parents. If teachers are going to innovate—to lead change, set new learning goals, and embed real context-based reform into their core work—building trust is an essential cornerstone.

Caught in the Squeeze

There's more to any story of successful classroom change, however. Increasingly, teachers' ability to manage their own curriculum, instruction, and assessment is being challenged by a growing infrastructure of state and federal accountability measures and fervent policymaking. Teachers who enter the profession bubbling with good ideas and a desire to change students' lives find they're expected to follow rigid instructional templates, ticking off benchmarks and goals set by people who never met the students in their classrooms.

In short, educators who want to generate custom-tailored, relevant, pioneering teaching in their classrooms are in a bind. School leaders are caught in the squeeze between following punitive top-down policy and doing what they know is best for students. New teachers, although enthusiastic about promoting change, often lack the experience and guidance to do so. And veteran teachers who want to stay in the classroom tread lightly around current waves of mandated reform.

Even prospective teachers are touched by the fallout. How many bright and creative people will the work of teaching attract if there's no opportunity for professional discretion and autonomy?

More Than a Technician

So how can we engender the kind of focused education leadership that will produce truly inventive teaching and deeper learning? How can teachers fulfill their aspirations of making a difference in their students' lives?

The answer may lie in transforming teaching. Over the past two decades, there's been a great deal of thinking and writing about teacher leadership. Administrators have been encouraged to nurture teacher leadership as a means of delegating responsibility for reaching schoolwide achievement goals. National alternate-entry programs are built around the concept of developing lifelong education leaders rather than superb classroom practitioners.

To be sure, teacher leaders share their good ideas, mentor novices, and build learning communities. Sometimes they're selected for special hybrid roles. But what they don't always have is control over their own work—and that's the mark of a profession.

In his Pulitzer Prize–winning book, *The Social Transformation of American Medicine* (Basic Books, 1982), Paul Starr identifies three attributes of a true profession: the cognitive, the collegial, and the moral. It's hard to see teaching as a profession in a policy atmosphere in which teachers' core tasks—developing curriculum, using assessment to inform instruction, working with parents, and upholding public education for the purpose of creating an educated citizenry—are controlled by forces outside their school and classroom. Teachers' hard-won cognitive expertise, collegial practices, and moral vision of education as an investment in equity are all under fire. In fact, we're moving away from teacher professionalism toward a teacher-as-technician model.

Take a look at this description of creative teaching by educator Shawn McCusker:

> One analogy for the role of the teacher in an abundant economy of information is that of the conductor. . . . The conductor may never play a single note, but his understanding of each small part of the larger work makes a far more powerful product possible. This is also true of the classroom teacher in the new economy of information. Group work can be assigned and completed, but the classroom teacher must . . . recognize the potential of the individual work that the students do and unite it together into a greater and more powerful work. When information is available in abundance, teachers will still be subject matter experts, but their true value will lie in their ability to facilitate and share the expertise of their students.[1]

Sound delicious? It's a great analogy for an ecology of practice that taps student strengths, embeds content knowledge seamlessly, and places instruction and curriculum decisions squarely in the classroom—with a teacher who's both an expert facilitator and a committed partner in learning. If these are the kinds of educators we want, however, we aren't going to get them by handing teachers predetermined benchmarks, scripts, and pacing charts, then monitoring their students' test scores for success.

Turning Teaching into a Profession

It will take a reconceptualization of our beliefs about teachers and teaching to accomplish the goal of creating a professional teaching force—a real sea change. Although such a shift may seem idealistic, other nations have been able to transform societal perspectives on what good teaching looks like, with skillful teachers taking professional responsibility for their students.

Classroom teachers in the United States, however, remain at the end of the decision-making funnel, their moral reasons for pursuing teaching compromised by tangled policy.

What would happen if teaching and learning were the primary consideration in all education policy, research, and funding? What if we didn't measure *teacher* effectiveness, but focused on *teaching* for a change? What if

- Designing curriculum were informed by teacher judgment about developmental appropriateness, student engagement, and the best tools to reach content standards?
- Standards for teaching practice were developed around performance in the classroom, rather than credentialing or standardized testing outcomes?
- Teacher evaluation included periodic on-site peer review for all teachers, novice and veteran, with an eye toward improving practice? What if teachers developed portfolios filled with evidence of their impact on student learning to share with colleagues?
- Professional development were selected and created by practitioners themselves? What if lively dialogue about education issues affecting their students were a regular feature of each day, informed by teachers' own scholarship and experience?
- Mentoring and induction programs were established with graduated responsibilities for novices?
- Teachers themselves guided the reshaping of the daily work of schools, including issues of scheduling, differentiated staffing, nonstandard calendars, hiring, and negotiating the use of available resources?
- Incentives were established to encourage K–12 teachers to write and speak publicly on crucial issues in education and do action research, creating an ethos of discourse and debate? What if every teacher were expected to contribute to this collective knowledge?

None of these requires comprehensive legislative change or significant reallocation of resources. It would be possible—in a generation, perhaps—to completely restructure teaching as a genuine profession, one school or district at a time.

Start Now

So how can teachers become professional change agents? I would suggest that teachers themselves are the only ones who can lead a movement toward articulating and demonstrating the complexity, importance, and power of creative teaching in improving the lives of the children we teach.

We can do more than just imagine a culture of innovation. We can take small steps every day toward demonstrating those cognitive, collegial, and moral behaviors of professionalism by

- Consciously making time for the big picture in education and staying abreast of issues of practice and policy. It's just as important for teachers to be familiar with the impact of national trends—the Common Core State Standards or the debate over teacher preparation, for example—as it is for them to be cognizant of in-school issues.
- Developing personal learning networks. Social media makes it possible to share ideas and opinions with teachers around the globe, clarify issues, and build well-researched plans for change. Facebook, Twitter, online publications, and disciplinary networks are rich resources for lesson ideas as well as advocacy.
- Working with on-site allies. The process of identifying others who are equally passionate about the work of teaching is exhilarating. When educators do take action, it's important not to be alone or isolated.
- Publicly demonstrating our commitment to students and our passion for their deeper learning every day. Teachers are first

responders when practice shifts. Their observations about new programs, assessment models, and curricular requirements are valuable and should be solicited and presented at school board meetings, at parent gatherings, and in publications.

- Gathering the courage to speak, and keep speaking, as experts. Few teachers enter the profession with the goal of becoming a public advocate, but avoiding public conversations about the work of teaching and learning doesn't serve children or the community well.

Trust is a resource, too—one that teachers can cultivate in their schools and communities and then use as a springboard for positive change. Relationships built on trust and expertise are at the heart of what it means to be a professional, and they enable us to move forward with confidence as change makers.

Endnote

[1] McCusker, S. (2014, April 7). Teachers' most powerful role? Adding context [blog post]. Retrieved from *Mind/Shift* at http://blogs.kqed.org/mindshift/2014/04/teachers-most-powerful-role-adding-context

Nancy Flanagan (nflanagan@centurylink.net) is an education writer and consultant focusing on teacher leadership. She blogs for *EdWeek* at *Teacher in a Strange Land*.

Originally published online in the June 2014 issue of *Educational Leadership*, 71: pp. 34–38.

Teaching Is Leading

Michelle Collay

Teacher leadership happens every day, both inside and outside the classroom.

Why do we feel that we need to apply the word *leader* to only certain teachers? One reason is that most of us think of a leader as someone who takes on additional roles outside the classroom. The perception that "regular" teachers are not leaders is reinforced by historical patterns of school management, such as physical isolation, exclusion of teachers from decision-making roles, and the chronic de-skilling of teachers through a constant barrage of misguided mandates (Cochran Smith & Lyttle, 2006).

Yet effective teaching *is* leadership. Leadership in schools means holding fast to a vision of democratic learning communities and taking actions, small and large, to disrupt inequity and to create real opportunities for students, families, colleagues, and community members. And in spite of inadequate funding, social factors that limit teacher professionalism, and outdated school structures, effective teaching and learning happen in all kinds of schools every day, as teachers lead by leveraging relationships within and beyond their classrooms.

Leading from the Classroom

Teachers lead by using their professional knowledge and judgment to support the learning of all students, by guiding the professional development of colleagues, and by participating in communities of practice (Barth, 2001; Danielson, 2006; Donaldson, 2007). Teaching is a vocation requiring everyday acts of leadership—courage, a clear vision of what matters, strong relationships with others, and resistance to the bureaucracy that can grind teachers down.

The following four dimensions of powerful classroom-based leadership are exemplified by 50 experienced teachers working in some of the most challenging urban districts in the United States (Collay, 2011). As program director and instructor in a teacher leadership master's degree program, I documented these experienced teachers' reflections about leadership over five years. I visited their classrooms, observed their courage and efficacy in action, and witnessed what transformative teacher leaders do.

Teachers Lead by Teaching Well

Teaching well means embracing the tensions of being in relationship with students, colleagues, parents, and the community (Gergen, 2009). Teaching is a messy business, requiring us to be theoretically grounded and purposeful while we respond to the ups and downs of the school day: providing one student with more structure and another student with less; staying in at lunchtime with a recalcitrant student in one case and sending her out for extra recess in another.

Those who teach are quite conscious of the countless decisions that influence relationships and build connections that lead to learning. Such intricate and subtle decision making requires professional expertise.

Teaching has been compared to jazz improvisation (Cuban, 2011), and like jazz musicians, teachers draw on deep knowledge of the art, technique, and emotional work of making meaning together. Here are some examples of how teachers lead by establishing and nurturing relationships:

- Sheila finds out that a student failing her English class will be kicked off the soccer team because of his low grades. She meets with the soccer coach and student to brainstorm some ways to raise his English grade.
- When Richard e-mails the parents of one of his high-performing students because she has stopped turning in homework, he discovers that her mother has been deployed with the National Guard. He asks the student to come by his room one morning each week so that they can send her mother updates. He also uses the sessions to check her homework and provide tutoring.
- Cristina has noticed a pattern of bullying by a group of 8th grade girls. She refers them to the guidance counselor, as required by school policy, but in her own classroom she also assigns each of them to tutor an English language learner. She meets with the girls weekly to learn about their tutees' progress.

Teachers Lead by Collaborating

Teacher collaboration with students, families, and colleagues is essential to create conditions for learning. Unlike directing a meeting or managing a staff, this collaboration is often invisible. School cultures and physical structures—from policies that forbid teachers to leave their classrooms unsupervised to long hallways that separate staff members from one another—often limit collaboration among adults. The very act of talking with a colleague during the day can be an accomplishment.

Teachers overcome such boundaries in creative ways, including developing study groups or professional learning communities. They lobby the school administration for designated prep time, use that time for relevant work, use emerging technologies to communicate, meet outside school, and find and share resources. But this kind of collaboration takes persistence (Collay, Dunlap, Enloe, & Gagnon, 1998).

Schooling traditions also limit collaboration between parents and teachers. Teacher–parent collaboration is evident in many elementary classrooms, typically decreases by middle school, and virtually disappears in high school. Partnering with parents can be fraught with tension on both sides, but some teachers seem to have a knack for building trust with even the most anxious parent or caretaker. It takes additional courage and leadership to share the path of coteaching and coparenting when divisions of race, language, and class complicate the relationship (Keyes, 2000; Miretsky, 2004).

Communication with parents is essential in teachers' efforts to make sense of students' lives within and beyond the classroom, a capacity that is often underrated and overlooked, even by teachers themselves. As a parent of two school-age children, my main concern at the parent conference is, Does this teacher *see* my child? What I'm really asking is, Does this important adult in my child's life know her as a whole person, with all her warts and gifts, or is she just a name in the grade book? The quality of their relationship has a profound influence on the quality of her learning.

The following examples show how teachers lead by building connections within and beyond the classroom:

- Dan calls three parents each night and shares something positive about their child.
- Maria organizes a term-long literacy project requiring her 5th graders to write reviews of Newbery Award books for primary students, interview primary teachers about their literacy curriculum, suggest age- and topic-appropriate chapter books, and volunteer as readers in the primary teachers' classrooms. The 5th graders send their reviews to the books' authors.
- Philomina arranges for students from her 7th grade life science classes to participate in a local nonprofit group's "Save

the Creek" clean-up event. In preparation, they study urban watershed ecology in class, interview a local ecologist from the Environmental Protection Agency, and e-mail members of the nonprofit group about examples of successful trout reintroduction in the same watershed. Students joining the clean-up receive a membership in the nonprofit group, and skeptical neighbors now see students from the local middle school as an asset to the community.
- Tai uses resources available through the California History–Social Science Project to take high school students through a study of their family's journey to or across North America. Each student interviews an immigrant from his or her ethnic or language community, often a family member. The videotaped interview and key events of that family's and ethnic group's journey are portrayed on a web-based timeline, with audio explanations provided in two languages. The materials are made available at the community library and arc used by teachers of English as a second language for their adult literacy classes.

Teachers Lead Through Inquiry

Studies conducted by education researchers often use "scientific" research methods that exclude the important factor of relationships between students and teachers. But classrooms are not laboratories, and students are not rats (fortunately). Classrooms are communities of practice, some more evolved than others. Measuring student "outcomes" on standardized tests provides *some* information about what students know, but it captures only a small part of a larger picture of complex, socially constructed knowledge.

When teachers lead through inquiry, they must begin with asking the right questions. Teachers must learn to trust their instincts, develop their own questions, deliberately document what they observe, and determine what action is needed. The hard-won knowledge they glean from such inquiry can empower them to hold their ground in the face of the next mandate or initiative. Thus, classroom-based inquiry is a requirement for good teaching and learning, not a luxury.

Formal teacher-led inquiry may include asking specific questions about how students learn: for example, conducting a child-study of one student's emotional development or comparing the progress of early readers who experience a new reading program with the progress of past cohorts of early readers. In addition, teachers conduct multiple forms of informal inquiry every day—from observing that a student is acting withdrawn and unhappy as he arrives at school to glancing at students' math tests and noting that almost the whole class missed problem 23. In the first case, the teacher may draw on her knowledge of the child, the family, and the school to sensitively explore why the student is upset and to respond constructively. In the second case, the teacher uses her awareness of curriculum flaws, knowledge of effective instruction, and interpretation of test results to conclude that students did not understand the material and she must teach it in a different way.

Here are some examples of teachers leading through inquiry:

- Jessie, Andrea, Jake, and Melissa are differentiating a math curriculum for middle school pre-algebra. Their department adopted a lesson-study framework for professional development. These teachers meet weekly to review their lesson plans, critique one another's instruction, and collect and organize unit assessment data. They observe and discuss one teacher's lesson each month. They record their observations of students' engagement with the math materials, collect assessment data from their own students, and use the test scores to identify target areas for instruction.
- A school implements Response to Intervention (RTI) to differentiate instruction for its students. Although grade-level teams agree that the concept has merit, even experienced teachers

are challenged to find time and space for assessing students and adapting their instruction. In addition to following the required protocol for identifying students and documenting their progress, grade-level teams use their shared prep time to discuss the challenges they have encountered and to strategize about the logistics of making RTI work. They invite the school's data coach to facilitate the development of student case studies, which they use to analyze individual students' strengths as learners, to compare writing samples from early efforts to final drafts, and to assess the fluency of English language learners. This enables them to form a comprehensive portrayal of student ability and to design instruction accordingly.

Teachers Lead by Developing Partnerships

Some partnerships are teacher-initiated, as productive teachers embrace expertise beyond the classroom and school. Teachers must also navigate partnerships that are not of their own making, such as those resulting from a mandate, a reform effort, or an external grant.

Good teaching in the context of either a welcome or an uninvited partnership requires a strategic response to the resources provided. Although experienced teachers may hold a healthy and understandable skepticism when told that this next initiative is "the answer," such skepticism should not keep them from taking advantage of useful parts of a grant, such as a coaching framework or materials that can improve learning in their classrooms. Good teaching unfolds when teachers broker resources for their students, strengthen existing collaborations within their schools, and build relationships with individuals who can provide relevant support.

For example, a nonprofit preschool agency in the county established a formal partnership with one elementary school's preschool staff. The agency provided training and resources for preschool teachers—including curriculum materials and manipulatives for math and language literacy—and trained staff to supervise recreation time. The preschool funding formula initially excluded kindergarten and 1st grade teachers Jamilla and Eduardo, who had worked with the preschool team to establish program coherence. Together, the preschool and primary staff asked the program director to include the primary grades in the initiative. This potentially divisive partnership now supports a reliable sequence of learning experiences for children ages 3–8, strengthening early literacy development.

Looking at Teaching Through the Lens of Leadership

It takes courage to trust our intuition, observations, and interpretations and to take action in the face of outside pressures and little support. But teachers lead every day by teaching well, collaborating with others, conducting well-designed inquiry, and forming partnerships. We should not underestimate the powerful leadership role played by teachers who build relationships from their classrooms outward, thus transforming themselves, their students, their students' families, their colleagues, and their communities.

References

Barth, R. (2001). Teacher leader. *Phi Delta Kappan, 82*(6), 443–449.

Cochran-Smith, M., & Lytle, S. (2006). Troubling images of teaching in No Child Left Behind. *Harvard Educational Review, 76*, 668–697.

Collay, M. (2011, June 16). *Everyday teacher leadership: Taking action where you are.* San Francisco: Jossey-Bass.

Collay, M., Dunlap, D., Enloe, W., & Gagnon, G. (1998). *Learning circles: Creating conditions for teacher professional development.* Thousand Oaks, CA: Corwin.

Cuban, L. (2011). Jazz, basketball, and teacher decision-making [blog post] Retrieved from *Larry Cuban on School Reform and Classroom Practice* at http://larrycuban.wordpress.com/2011/06/16/jazz-basketball-and-teacher-decision-making

Danielson, C. (2006). *Teacher leadership that strengthens professional practice.* Alexandria, VA: ASCD.

Donaldson, G. (2007). What do teachers bring to leadership? *Educational Leadership, 65*(1), 26–29.

Gergen, K. (2009). *Relational being: Beyond self and community.* Oxford, UK: Oxford University Press.

Keyes, C. (2000). Parent-teacher partnerships: A theoretical approach for teachers. *Issues in early childhood education: Curriculum, teaching education, and dissemination of information* (Proceedings of the Lilian Katz Symposium, Champaign, Illinois). Retrieved from http://ecap/crc/illinois.edu/pubs/katzsym/keyes.pdf

Miretsky, D. (2004). The communication requirements of democratic schools: Parent-teacher perspectives on their relationships. *Teachers College Record, 106,* 814–851.

Michelle Collay (mcollay@une.edu) is director of the Online Doctoral Program in Educational Leadership, University of New England, Biddeford and Portland, Maine. She is the author of *Everyday Teacher Leadership: Taking Action Where You Are* (Jossey-Bass, 2011).

Originally published in the October 2013 issue of *Educational Leadership, 71*(2): pp. 72–76.

Now That I Know What I Know

Dan Brown

Looking back at his first disastrous year of teaching, a veteran shares what he's learned.

It takes a village to raise a competent teacher, but I didn't know that as a rookie.

Descending P.S. 85's stairs to pick up my students on September 8, 2003, my first day as a real 4th grade teacher in the Bronx, I thought I had things figured out. I was 22 and newly graduated from New York University, a prestigious institution where—just as in high school—I'd earned top grades. The New York City Teaching Fellows, a selective alternative certification program, had accepted my application and deemed me qualified to teach in a high-needs public school. Up to then, I'd done pretty well as a student, so I expected that teaching—just a stone's throw from studenthood, I thought—would offer me a similar equation:

effort + intelligence + people skills = success

I loved kids, had a career-teacher mom, and was willing to dedicate myself full-time to my students. How wrong could it go?

Once my kids and I arrived in the classroom, I talked at them about teamwork, rules, and respect. They looked at me while I delivered my speech, a response that I interpreted as tacit and complete agreement with everything I had said. A few students even spoke up to define respect and provide real-life examples. Their participation elated me, and I let them know it with fist bumps and celebratory hand gestures.

About 45 minutes into my teaching career, Fausto, a boy I'd been warned about in the faculty lounge, stood up from the reading rug during my reading of Taro Yashima's *Crow Boy* and wandered toward the door. The other students went silent, watching me confront the first brazen challenge to my authority.

It didn't go well. Fausto's shout of "This story wack yo!" drew raucous laughter, and I doused gasoline on the flames by replying, "The story is *not* wack. Are you ready to stop acting like a kindergartner?"

I never finished the sentence. The class had already degenerated into a whooping fracas ("Mr. Brown said *wack!*"), and I gracelessly scrambled to silence everyone. My desperation was obvious, the calm from moments before irrevocably lost.

The remaining 99.9 percent of the school year felt defined by this initial blunder. I perpetually battled uphill to gain command of the class, an often fruitless effort. Instead of teaching fractions, I struggled to avert fisticuffs.

I scratched out minor victories as the year wore on, but my students hadn't learned nearly as much as I aspired to teach them. Our classroom didn't resemble school as I had experienced it as a youngster. If my own daughter had been in that turbulent environment, I'd have had a heart attack. At the end of the school year I resigned, joining the legions of teachers who bolt the profession in their first years. I was sure that my initial power struggle with Fausto had cost the class a stable school year.

More Than Just Jumping In

I did return to teaching a year later, determined to get it right. Since then, and especially after the release of *The Great Expectations School*, my memoir about that rookie year, I've shared in dozens of conversations with educators and stakeholders about how to mitigate the steep learning curve of new teachers. Invariably the question comes up, Now that you know what you know, what would you have done differently on that first morning in the Bronx?

For a long time, I offered convoluted answers about classroom management systems or not letting the students see me sweat, but the truth is, I didn't really know. I was still looking at the Fausto debacle as a personal failure, through the lens of my equation for success that had served me as a student when the variables were all within my control. As a new teacher, I had approached my job with the same mind-set: I'm the authority figure in the classroom. I deserve the credit or the blame if my effort, intelligence, and people skills succeed or fail.

But as a new teacher, you don't know what you don't know. My grit and wit alone couldn't bring about a positive 4th grade year for my students. I had bought into the fallacy—propagated by the marketing for my alternative certification program—that basically anybody smart and willing can jump in and do this.

A New Equation for Staying Afloat

Now with a master's degree, years of experience, and National Board certification, I realize that a much more accurate equation for a teacher's success encompasses a sea of factors. The first three I list are within the teacher's control; the rest are not. The absence of any of these elements risks sinking the whole ship, as I learned in the Bronx.

Comfort with Your Teacher Persona

As Dan, I don't really care if a kid tucks in his shirt. As Mr. Brown, little matters more. As Dan, I utter a curse word every now and then. As Mr. Brown, foul language offends me deeply.

You can't entirely be yourself as a teacher; you have to cultivate a *teacher persona*—a blend of your real self and the benevolent pedagogical manipulator and authority figure that teachers must be. Kids can sense phoniness or fear; they certainly sniffed out and exploited my greenness on that first day in the Bronx. Losing your composure in front of students is bad, bad news. Many young people have a perverse desire to push their teachers' buttons; if you wear them on your sleeve, they're going to get pushed. My nascent teacher persona was a panicked one. I screamed at my students several times in my rookie year. When I did, I accomplished my short-term goal of achieving momentary silence but wreaked unknowable damage to my hopes for a nurturing team atmosphere.

Finding and embracing one's teacher persona takes time and practice. It's especially hard for new graduates venturing for the first time into the professional sector, when they are often charged with teaching students only a little younger than they are. Still, it's an important realization for new teachers to make—that they must build a hybrid between their authentic personalities and their roles as professional educators. The best way to do this is to closely observe and reflect on a variety of teachers in action, then try out some of their strategies.

It all boils down to coming across as well-organized and kind—these are the two qualities that stand out to students more than any other. To get there, follow the first teaching standard from the National Board for Professional Teaching Standards, which is "knowledge of students." The first part of that is learning students' names as soon as is humanly possible. New teachers have a lot on their plates, but all is for naught if you offend a student two weeks into the year by blanking on her name.

Familiarity with the School Community

In the Bronx, my classroom was my fiefdom—Mr. Brown's room. It was the one place where I was in charge. I loved shutting my door on all the outside unpleasantness. I believed that if I could just get my room under control, I'd be on top.

This was an incomplete view of a teacher's role. Teachers, especially rookies, shouldn't be islands. Relationships among adults beyond the classroom walls make all the difference in a school. This includes administrators and colleagues, of course—but also parents.

Parents need to feel good about communicating with the teacher; new teachers need to present themselves as available and welcoming. Especially in low-income areas, some new teachers' negative preconceptions about parents of "these kids" can be highly damaging. Phone calls, e-mails, and conversations on the blacktop are very important. Indeed, a standard for every National Board certificate is "partnerships with colleagues, families, and the community." Not every outreach to a parent will bear visible fruit in a student's performance in class, but then again, teachers often don't see the full fruits of their labors. We plant seeds and are delighted when we see a real payoff in a student's growth.

Dedication to the Job

I wasn't used to failure when I stepped into my first teaching job—and it stung. Part of persevering in this profession involves carrying a high threshold for bureaucratic blunders, miscarriages of justice, untimely copy machine malfunctions, misguided policies, betrayals of trust, and other epic travesties—as well as one's own mistakes.

Being a dedicated teacher means picking your battles where you can and fighting them hard. One battle new teachers can always wage is with their own inexperience with lesson planning. On paper, my job in the Bronx was to teach several subjects to my homeroom of 26 4th graders between 8 a.m. and 3 p.m. At first, I wrote up lesson plans on the template I'd been given and arrived at school determined to stick to them. They were my bedrock.

The reality is that as a teacher, you make countless decisions each day. The act of crafting and executing a lesson plan is like creating a delicately nuanced work of art—infinite adjustments based on your knowledge of your students are necessary. The ability to reflect and adapt your takeaways to the next lesson is what separates teachers who are getting stronger in their craft from those who are treading water, going nowhere.

School leaders should provide opportunities for collaboration between rookies and veterans, where new teachers can test out their plans, learn about good practices, and be observed in the classroom. However, if the school structure doesn't make space on the schedule for these connections, it's crucial to make them happen underground. Novice teachers can only figure out so much on their own. Dedication to the job means forging relationships and creating opportunities to pick colleagues' brains, figure out what works, and apply it to your class.

New teachers can be easily demoralized. Failure hurts, and the mixed messages in education can be baffling. Teachers are caught in a paradox of buzz phrases; they're pressured to "meet students where they are" while "setting high expectations for all." Idealistic preservice teachers tend to believe strongly in the latter, only to be confounded with how to handle real live students with skill levels all over the map.

Real dedication means working to differentiate instruction and never throwing up one's hands. I didn't understand this at my induction. The dedication and vigor I'd imagined in myself before starting the school year became much harder to marshal once my best-laid plans fell to pieces.

High-Quality Preparation Programs

The first time I spent more than an hour in a functioning classroom during the regular school year, I was put in charge of it—a setup for failure. The alternative certification model of several weeks of frantic summer training instilled in me more terror than confidence.

Teaching is an art and a science, and it takes a lot of time to figure out. Extensive observation and student teaching must be a bare minimum before any teacher tries to run a classroom. I doubt that any policymakers would welcome their child being taught by an underprepared alternative certification rookie.

Models of success outside the traditional graduate school route exist. The Urban Teacher Residency United, with partner programs in Boston, Chicago, Denver, and several other U.S. cities, is a revelation in teacher preparation. Recruits spend a full school year as apprentice teachers learning the craft. It's expensive; districts invest in the future teachers by subsidizing stipends and offering graduate-level coursework for highly motivated career changers. The program works. The coalition's website reports that 85 percent of residents remain in the classroom after their first three years, compared with 50 percent of urban teachers who have not participated in this program. The extra preparation time makes all the difference.

Supportive School Leaders

In the Bronx, my principal showed no interest in developing her staff. She addressed the faculty as "you people" in meetings and frequently cut colleagues off in conversation. The assistant principals took cues from her.

For much of my first year, the sight of administrators filled me with dread. The idea that they could help me become a better teacher was not even a passing thought; they were menaces to avoid. When my class teetered into chaos, I had no idea whether I could count on the higher-ups to help; sometimes they would undermine me with public castigation. One administrator told me the day before school started, "Don't need us too much, especially in the beginning. Prove you can handle yourself."

I'm currently in my fourth year at the SEED Public Charter School in Washington, D.C. Head of School Charles Adams and Principal Kara Stacks are both in their fifth years, and they are energetic, supportive former teachers. Under their leadership, staff turnover is low, and the continuity they have engendered is invaluable to the school culture. Test scores are also way up, but not because of drilling; it's a natural by-product of a higher-functioning community.

Adams and Stacks have also supported me in forming external partnerships with such local organizations as the Shakespeare Theatre Company and the PEN/Faulkner Society. These connections have been invaluable in exposing students to cultural opportunities and boosting student learning. It's energizing when my school leaders encourage me to try new stuff.

Kids in my class are now far less likely to freak out than my 4th graders in the Bronx were, but if they do, both the students and I know the exact consequences and chain of command for dealing with it. For better or worse, administrators mold the culture of the school.

High-Quality Curriculum

High-stakes testing and its attendant army of prepackaged test-prep curriculum vendors are waging a formidable campaign to tear the soul out of public education. It's up to educators to fight this and make sure that standardized assessment is a tool, not a way of life. However, new teachers have virtually no clout when it comes to their curriculum.

Scripted curriculums are boring for students and teachers. People don't have breakthroughs or epiphanies, and it's deadening for intellectual curiosity. In the Bronx, test-prep season dominated several months—it wasn't what I'd signed up for. The idea of facing another school year with that pressure-cooker tension over testing was a factor in my decision to leave.

Conversely, a high-quality curriculum activates students' and teachers' curiosity and individual gifts. And there's so much exciting and empowering stuff out there. Administrators who choose scripted test prep are operating from a position of fear. I wouldn't want my kid in one of their schools. I also wouldn't want to teach there.

District Policies That Promote Good Teaching

Some people in power obsess over cosmetic things—like bulletin boards. This was the case my rookie year, when the regional superintendent was universally feared for her penchant for visiting classrooms hours before school opened, photographing your bulletin boards, and putting stinging critiques of them in your permanent file.

Even worse, the craze over high-stakes test scores has forced schools to distort budgets, schedules, and curriculums in a thousand ways. New teachers can't thrive when their supervisors' priorities do not involve excellent teaching.

District administrators need to hire strong school leaders, get them what they need, and stay out of their way. Part of what they need is high-quality professional development that directly applies to work with students, fosters collaboration, and stretches out much longer than a single drive-by experience.

Don't Forget the Village

For each of these factors, it's crucial for veteran teachers and school leaders to build the infrastructure to support new teachers' success. Rookies don't grow into strong teachers if they're in hostile environments or under attack.

Trial by fire isn't fair for anyone. For me in the Bronx, this approach invited Fausto to make a bombastic test of my authority and consigned 25 other students to education purgatory when his challenge exposed my inexperience.

New teachers can't do it alone, but with supportive leaders, student-centered policies, solid curriculum, and opportunities to learn their craft and connect with the community, they'll be in a position to earn those student breakthroughs and experience those epiphanies that provide the rocket fuel to continue and improve.

Dan Brown (danbrownteacher@gmail.com) teaches 11th and 12th grade English at the SEED Public Charter School of Washington, D.C. He is the author of *The Great Expectations School: A Rookie Year in the New Blackboard Jungle* (Skyhorse Publishing, 2011). Follow him @danbrownteacher on Twitter.

Originally published in the May 2012 issue of *Educational Leadership*, 69(8): pp. 24–28.

Edcamp: Teachers Take Back Professional Development

Kristen Swanson

How can participant-led, one-day events open up new possibilities for professional learning?

"I have heard more positive feedback on this day than any other professional development I have ever been a part of. I keep wondering why we didn't take our professional development in this direction a lot earlier. If we want classrooms where we are teaching students to be collaborative and more proactive in their learning, don't we have to set up a culture where we trust teachers to do the same?"

—Patrick Larkin (2010), assistant superintendent

Hundreds of quotes like this one have been circulating within the Twittersphere and Blogosphere since May 2010. What's all the buzz about? Edcamp.

How Did Edcamp Begin?

Edcamps are free, participatory events organized by educators for educators. Attendees collaboratively determine the schedule of sessions on the morning of the event. The first Edcamp was organized by a group of educators (including me) after we met in September 2009 at BarCamp Philly, an unconference focused on technology. After experiencing the passion, sharing, and excitement that surrounded that event, we wanted to develop a similar learning model for teachers and administrators. We exchanged contact information, and over the next few months, communicating through virtual dialogue and several Skype meetings, we hammered out a vision of Edcamps. Operating on a shoestring budget, we advertised our first Edcamp event through Twitter, Facebook, word of mouth, and blogs. Within a few months, more than 100 people had signed up to attend.

On an unseasonably cool morning in May 2010, lots of educators arrived at the Philadelphia location, collaboratively built a schedule of sessions related to their interests, and talked. And talked. And talked. Several of the sessions focused on best practices, a few shared successful lessons, and others explored Web 2.0 tools. Overall, it was a positive, interactive day. Personally, I couldn't recall another professional learning experience where I got to do so much discussing and sharing.

Exhausted and elated, the organizing team met that night to debrief. Almost as an afterthought, Dan Callahan suggested creating a free Wikispace to document the experience online.

And so it began. As people who had attended the first Edcamp started to share their experience online via blogs and Twitter, interest grew. Slowly, e-mails and tweets began to arrive asking how to do what we had done. One of the original organizers, Mary Beth Hertz (2010), published a four-part blog series on our experiences. Soon new Edcamp events started popping up. In the last four years, more than 400 Edcamps have been held all over the United States and in other countries.

What Does a Day at an Edcamp Look Like?

It's difficult to capture the Edcamp experience. That's because a "typical" day of learning at an Edcamp doesn't really exist. Each Edcamp is based on the needs of its participants.

When you arrive at the location (usually a school or university), there is no preset schedule of sessions or presenters. Instead, there's just a big, blank sheet of paper with a grid on it.

From that blank slate, everyone builds the schedule together. As people mingle and chat over coffee and doughnuts, they put up potential discussion topics on a board. The entire process is positive and organic. Occasionally, people who don't even know each other realize they have similar interests and end up running a session together. Other folks come with an idea, throw it out to the group, revise it, and post it with a refined focus. Because anyone who attends an Edcamp event can be a presenter, it's an empowering experience for everyone.

Given the spontaneity of the schedule creation, you may wonder about the content of the sessions that typically occur at an Edcamp. It's certainly hard to generalize, but here is a sampling of topics presented at recent Edcamp events:

- Engagement, Respect, and Reciprocity in Public/Private School Partnerships.
- We Taught 6th Graders Quantum Physics with Dance.
- How to Address Privacy and One's Digital DNA.
- Design Thinking and Innovation.
- Writing in the Digital Age.

Sessions at Edcamp are diverse and eclectic because they grow out of the interests and expertise of the participants. However, the participants themselves also actively control the quality of each session via the "law of two feet" (Boule, 2011), which states that participants in an Edcamp session can leave the room at any time for any reason. Because leaving midstream is actually encouraged, sessions with weak content or too much presenter talk often end up sparsely populated, whereas high-quality, interactive sessions are often bursting at the seams.

Most sessions are informal conversations or demonstrations. It's common for many different people to take the floor during an event to share an idea, show student work on their laptop, or ask questions. In short, the experience is closer to a vibrant summer camp than a routine day of conference sessions.

The Edcamp day ends with a "Smackdown," during which any willing participant takes the floor for 30 seconds to share an idea, tool, or tip with the crowd. There's typically music, laughing, and cheering as folks try to condense their learning into such a small time frame.

Although Edcamps are not specifically about technology, many teachers who run and attend Edcamps are comfortable with it. Edcamps also run back channels on Twitter during the event to encourage participants to chat virtually *while* the live discussions happen. For example, Edcamp LA had 1,587 tweets during the daylong event. (You can see the entire archive.) People use the back channel to communicate, share links, and draw people who aren't physically present into the conversation. So although technology is not a required part of the model, it certainly helps spread and capture the learning of the day.

Edcamp How-To

How to Attend an Event

If you're interested in attending an Edcamp event, check the Edcamp wiki for the complete calendar of events. Visit the page of the event you wish to attend and register for a free ticket. Most attendees bring a laptop or tablet to the event so they can share resources and ideas in the back channel. Go to the event with ideas and expertise to share!

How to Organize an Event

Anyone can run an Edcamp event. Here are seven recommended steps for success.

Find 3–5 like-minded educators who are interested in running an Edcamp event with you. Maybe these people work in your school or teach in your area, or perhaps you are connected through a social network, such as Facebook or Twitter. Regardless of where you find your team, as long as they're passionate educators you're all set.

Check the Edcamp wiki to learn about other Edcamp events that have happened in your area. Reach out to these organizers through e-mail to learn from their experience. It can also be helpful to attend an Edcamp before trying to run one. This will help you visualize what your event could look like.

Find a venue and set a date. This is the hardest step. Most organizers get permission to use their school's facilities. Many places have donated space to Edcamp events, but be sure to check for hidden costs—for example, event insurance or custodial services. Your venue should have one large space where everyone can gather to build the schedule in the morning and to share experiences at the end of the day. It should also have 4–10 smaller breakout rooms to accommodate the different sessions. Free wireless access for all the participants is also important.

Get funding and sponsors as needed. If you need to pay for your event space, then you'll need some sponsors. It's best to start in your community with local education organizations. Organizations or businesses will often donate goods or services such as bagels, coffee, and T-shirts.

Tell everyone about your event. Create a logo, website, and Twitter account for your event. Add your event and logo to the Edcamp wiki. You can use Ticketleap or Eventbrite to give out free tickets and track registration. Expect about 40–60 percent of registrants to actually attend on the day of the event. (High attrition is one of the consequences of hosting a free event.)

Take care of the little things. Find a big piece of poster paper to use as your blank schedule board. Decide whether you'll provide snacks, lanyards, or other goodies for the attendees.

Host your amazing event. It's best to have 5–10 volunteers on hand to help with registration and the schedule as the day gets started. Enjoy the day of learning and growing!

A Growing Movement

The Edcamp model has spread rapidly since our first event in 2010, not only throughout the United States (41 states are now represented) but also internationally to Sweden, Ontario, British Columbia, Japan, Vietnam, Indonesia, Australia, Belgium, Abu Dhabi, Denmark, Hong Kong, Ukraine, and Chile. Fifty-one Edcamp events were held in 2011, 127 were held in 2012, and 190 were held in 2013. Some events focused on specific topics, such as leadership or new teacher induction. One Edcamp event was even organized by high school students for local educators.

The Edcamp wikispace currently has more than 1,200 organizing members, and hundreds of thousands of tweets have been written with the #edcamp hashtag. In an effort to address the growing number of educators with questions and requests for support, the original organizing team created the Edcamp Foundation in December 2011. This nonprofit organization has provided support to more than 125 Edcamps in places as near as Ohio and as far away as Hong Kong.

When we organized the original Edcamp in 2010, we never dreamed that this type of explosion would happen. That is the power of technology in education. It's not about the shiny production tools or neat gadgets. Instead, it's about connecting people with purpose and finding new ways to learn. Ideas can spread quickly, efficiently, and with fervor.

This shift could not have come at a better time. Mass media has not been kind to educators lately, and many teachers have lost their direction in a sea of mounting mandates and requirements. The relationships participants form at an Edcamp provide needed support and spark important new learning as these educators continue to dialogue long after the event is over. Most powerfully, lots of educators try new strategies they've learned at Edcamp and then report back to the Edcamp community on their blogs to get feedback and share progress.

For example, Craig Yen is an educator from California who has attended multiple Edcamps. At one, he learned about Mystery Skypes, in which students from two classrooms in different geographic locations exchange a series of questions through Skype, and each classroom tries to figure out where the other classroom (the "mystery callers") is located. This strategy can encourage global collaboration, widen students' perspectives, and hone their speaking and listening skills.

After returning to his classroom and trying Mystery Skypes with his 5th graders, Craig blogged about the experience and noted some technical problems he encountered and fixed. Overall, he deemed the experiment a success, writing, "We had some good questions from our side, for instance, 'Are you landlocked?' This made the kids think more about the different regions and geographical terms."

This extension of learning is what most participants cite as the most satisfying aspect of participant-led learning events. Andrea Keller (2012) writes, "The reason I am super excited about this is the connections that I make. They might be in person during the day, but they tend to be virtual after that."

Edcamps are also feeding the new need for instant information. In today's climate, pedagogies and tools change quickly. Edcamps have the flexibility to respond to these trends, giving educators the skills they need. For example, iBooks Author (an Apple publishing tool) came out just days before Edcamp UCLA in January 2012. Sure enough, teachers posted sessions about the tool, helping lots of educators stay abreast of its potential uses and pitfalls.

Trusting Teachers

In spite of the widespread growth of Edcamps, some educators remain skeptical about the format. People often ask me how "quality content" can be guaranteed. They're often surprised when I tell them, *You can't guarantee anything at an Edcamp.*

We have to trust that teachers are professionals who use their classrooms as innovative laboratories and who are motivated to engage in authentic learning. Although the "law of two feet" encourages participants to immediately abandon sessions that appear biased, of low quality, or less than useful, it's certainly not foolproof. Further, Edcamp events are only one component of a balanced professional learning diet. Teachers should also engage in rigorous reading, action research, and collaborative curriculum writing, among other things. However, when included as part of a balanced learning plan, Edcamps can empower and motivate teachers to learn and share powerful practices.

For me, attending an Edcamp reminds me that I'm part of something bigger. Education is greater than my classroom, school, or district. It's a powerful force that can bring equity and empowerment to our world.

Resources

Boule, M. (2011). Mob rule learning: Camps, unconferences, and trashing the talking head. New York: Information Today.

Hertz, M. (2010). Introduction to Edcamp: A new conference model built on collaboration [blog post]. Retrieved from Edutopia at www.edutopia.org/blog/about-edcamp-unconference-history

Keller, A. (2012, March 16). Energize … find a padcamp or edcamp [blog post]. Retrieved from Discovery Educator Network at http://blog.discoveryeducation.com/blog/2012/03/16/energize-find-an-padcamp-or-edcamp

Larkin, P. (2010, September 29). A professional development day that worked: A recap [blog post]. Retrieved from Burlington High School Principal's Blog at www.markjsullivan.org/2010/09/professional-development-day-that.html

---

Kristen Swanson (kristennicoleswanson@gmail.com) is senior educational research leader at BrightBytes, San Francisco, California. She is the author of *Professional Learning in the Digital Age* (Routledge, 2012) and *Teaching the Common Core Speaking and Listening Standards: Strategies and Digital Tools* (Routledge, 2013).

Originally published in the May 2014 issue of *Educational Leadership*, 71(8): pp. 36–40.

The Best Teachers I Have Known

Susan Allred

Whether they were teaching in the 1960s or in the 2000s, effective teachers share a common set of characteristics.

One of the joys of retirement is having the time to reflect on our profession. Looking back over the 37 years I spent as an educator—20 of them as a teacher and 17 as an administrator—and reflecting on my own schooling as well, I think of the many highly effective teachers I've known. Spanning all grade levels, they engaged students in learning to the point of excitement and kindled the desire to keep on learning.

So what did these teachers have in common?

They Were Masters of Their Content

All of these teachers knew their subject matter. The questions they raised with students made it clear that it was OK not to know the details, but *not* OK not to pursue the answers. These teachers were enthusiastic about their subject matter, as though what was going on at that moment was the most important thing ever. They connected their content to everything they did.

One school had a science class for gifted and talented students. The science teacher lived and breathed science. One morning when I arrived at school—at 5:30 a.m., as was my habit—a car was already parked out in front. In it were a sleepy-eyed father and his twin daughters who were in 4th grade. As I walked toward the car, the girls were already bounding out the door. The father rolled down his window and said, "I hope it's all right for me to bring them. They said you'd be here, and they're sure the chicks in the lab hatched overnight. They couldn't wait to come. You know, they help the science teacher in the lab every morning."

Actually, I didn't know that they helped the science teacher, who didn't teach either of the children, but I did know that she shared her love of science with all the students in the school. By the time school started, every 4th grader had already been in to see the chicks.

They Were Insatiable Learners

Perhaps the most frustrated classroom teachers I have worked with or observed were those who thought that four years of undergraduate training should carry them through a 30-year career. These teachers feel oppressed by professional development of any kind. Their mantra is, "Just give me my kids, and let me teach."

The most effective teachers realize that the world and students have changed since they completed their undergraduate work, and they look for opportunities to address the gaps in their knowledge and ability. A middle school teacher learned about a local astronomical research laboratory and what it might offer students. The school curriculum didn't have a regular focus on astronomy, but a single trip helped this teacher realize that a world-class resource was in her backyard. Connections with the institute enabled students to watch and program the satellite dishes from their classroom computers. Students were then able to use the data collected on weather, planets, and stars in their daily science lessons. A teacher's enthusiasm for her own new learning enhanced her classroom.

In the final district in which I worked, we implemented the Baldrige Management System for Performance Excellence. This quality-based system, which requires constant review of data and information, created angst among many teachers. Professional development on the system met with mixed reviews.

But one day, a special education teacher called me into her room. She asked a kindergarten student to tell me about his "chart." "I was supposed to learn 50 words by Christmas," he said. Then he pointed to the October column on his bar graph and exclaimed, "See, I've learned 50 already. I get to learn more!" The teacher hadn't learned to use this system in her undergraduate work. Even though she was somewhat skeptical about whether it would work, she had learned it because she thought it might help her students. And it did.

They Had a Positive Outlook

Not earning enough money; having too many students, too many meetings, and too many levels of learners; trying to satisfy challenging expectations; and often feeling like the first line of defense against pandemics, child abuse, and student drug use—these are enough to get anybody down. But despite all these factors, effective teachers believe that today is the best day ever—and that tomorrow will be even better.

One compassionate 3rd grade teacher I knew vigorously lobbied to take into her class 12 students with special needs whom we were attempting to fully include in the regular student population. Late in September, I asked her to take on still another student—a little Finnish girl who didn't speak English. Three months later, the child was communicating well in the class. Just before Christmas break, the teacher left a note on my desk that read, "I just wanted to thank you for my class. You've apologized so often for the pressure it puts on me. But I love the students, and they are learning so very much. I would not have wanted it any other way."

They Were Team Members

Effective teachers know they cannot do the work alone. With so much information available these days, we need the best brains to work collaboratively to pull solutions together. It really does take a village.

But in high school, it's often more difficult to get this point across. The math department at the high school in which I was assistant principal was especially effective in this area. The department had aligned the curriculum both vertically and horizontally. A record-keeping system in the math office kept teachers current with what students knew and what they needed to know to move to the next level of math.

In the three years I held that position, not a single student was unsuccessful in math. If math teachers saw a new trend in student performance data that identified gaps in learning—for example, students not mastering polynomials—the department would revise the sequence or content of courses. Moreover, the advanced placement calculus teacher had a 100-percent pass rate (3 or better on the exam) for many years. That was possible because the department was committed to preparing the students through course sequencing, by ensuring mastery of skills before moving forward—providing tutoring, for example, and giving students extra time—and by frequently meeting with students, parents, and other teachers about students' achievement.

We had the same success in tech prep math, our applied mathematics program. Two teachers teamed up during their lunch and planning time to hold a special lab for students who struggled to pass the state exam. For many years, those teachers also had a 100-percent success rate.

They Created Communities for Success

The teachers I have described not only knew the achievement levels of their students, but also made sure that students knew where they were, where they needed to be, and how they would get there. Moreover, they created an environment in which students felt empowered and valuable and in which they learned to respectfully appreciate the differences in the room.

Through modeling and by clarifying expectations regarding conduct and engagement, these teachers promoted respectful interaction of students in their classrooms that was nothing short of democracy in action. Students could be at any level of learning ability or from any ethnic or religious group; students accepted one another with their body piercings, Goth clothing, dyed hair, or native dress. The focus was on learning.

These effective teachers did what all effective teachers do—they established clear and high expectations and gave students some choice in how they would learn. For example, rather than going over each homework item, one high school teacher had a process for students to report the items that gave them trouble—students wrote these down on a white board as they entered the room. Those were the items that the teacher reviewed. Students also had homework buddies so that if they had extra time, they could begin doing their homework together. Students suggested both strategies.

Another teacher had her students list on a strategy board the things that helped them learn particular concepts. A regular part of the day focused on "what works" and on "what doesn't work as well." For example, one of the class's goals was that every student would earn 90 percent or better on the weekly vocabulary test. To help ensure this, the students decided to take their words to the lunch room and study them together after they finished eating. The weeks they used that strategy, the class met its goal. So the strategy went on the strategy board.

All This—And More

Of course, in addition to the characteristics I've mentioned, effective teachers display professionalism, are exceptional communicators with all stakeholders, and don't watch the clock. As I sit here rocking on my porch, I count myself fortunate to have known so many of them.

Susan Allred (susanallred@att.net) has spent 37 years in education, as both a teacher and administrator. Currently retired from public education, she now serves as an education consultant.

Originally published online in the June 2010 issue of *Educational Leadership, 67*.

Study Guide for *On Being a Teacher: Readings from* Educational Leadership

Naomi Thiers

Ideas to try out individually or in a study group.

Whether you're a new teacher, a veteran, or an administrator hoping to support your faculty, articles in this e-book will provide words of wisdom about the teaching profession. Here are questions and activities that will help you get the most out of the articles.

What Is Effective Teaching— and How Do We Get There?

Carol Ann Tomlinson ("Notes from an Accidental Teacher") discusses five practices that "make up the architecture of effective teaching." Consider two of these practices: (1) finding a teaching situation that fits you well and helps you grow and (2) "knowing what you don't know."

- Tell about a place where you taught that was a great fit and helped you blossom—and one that was a poor fit. What made the difference?

- Do you agree with Tomlinson's statement that "excellent teachers never fall prey to the belief that they are good enough"? Why or why not?

Many teachers now craft their *own* professional learning opportunities, even their own conferences. Many educators want conferences to be more than times to attend workshops led by big-name presenters. In fact, new models have cropped up that require educators to become active in planning and participating in the learning. Edcamp (described in "Edcamp: Teachers Take Back Professional Development" by Kristen Swanson) offers a new model for conducting a professional conference.

- Edcamp-style conferences depend on the active participation of educators who attend. Attendees are themselves the experts, and they learn from one another. What do you see as the benefits and drawbacks of this participant-driven approach? For what kinds of teacher learning might this model be best suited?
- What kinds of experiences do you most value at a professional conference? How would you change conferences to make them even more useful?

Supporting Brand New Teachers

Many teachers, like Dan Brown ("Now That I Know What I Know") find their first year as a teacher of record to be lonely and difficult. One element Brown says can make the first year easier is developing a teacher persona: "You can't entirely be yourself as a teacher; you have to cultivate a teacher persona—a blend of your real self and the benevolent pedagogical manipulator and authority figure that teachers must be."

- Do you agree that a teacher needs to forge such a persona? Consider this: have you created a teacher persona for yourself,

and if so, what is it like? How is it different from your non-school self?
- Think back to your first year as a teacher. What are some of your clearest memories? Do many of them involve feelings of failure or doubt? What's the first teaching triumph you remember
- In Marge Scherer's interview with noted educator Linda Darling-Hammond ("The Challenges of Supporting New Teachers"), Darling-Hammond talks about how crucial it is for new teachers to have "systematic, intense mentoring" in their first year. Share your experience of receiving (or not receiving) mentoring in your first year or two. How are new teachers mentored in your current school? How effective do you think that mentoring is?

Of Teacher Leaders and Change Agents

Reflect on Michelle Collay's ("Teaching Is Leading") assertion that all teachers are leaders within their classrooms:

> Teachers lead by using their professional knowledge and judgment to support the learning of all students, by guiding the professional development of colleagues, and by participating in communities of practice. . . Teaching is a vocation requiring everyday acts of leadership—courage, a clear vision of what matters, strong relationships with others, and resistance to the bureaucracy.

Making a space for teachers to be leaders *outside* their classrooms is also a great way for them to learn. In "The Problem-Solving Power of Teachers," Ariel Sacks makes a case for teacher leadership by sharing how teachers at her school could see the flaws in a schoolwide homework policy that looked good on paper but didn't work in practice.

The teachers came up with a way to adjust the policy so that it better benefited both students and teachers.

- What role do teachers at your school play in setting schoolwide policy on homework, discipline, and other issues? What's the value of bringing teachers into policy discussions? How might your school make better use of teacher voices when making decisions?
- If you're a teacher, have you ever had to implement a top-down policy that didn't work well in practice? How did you respond?

As Nancy Flanagan makes clear in her article in this collection ("Take Back Teaching Now"), she found that being a change agent requires courage, some ownership of the reforms you're pushing, and trustworthy allies. Flanagan notes that "If teachers are going to . . . lead change, set new learning goals, and embed real context-based reform into their core work—building trust is essential."

- Brainstorm ways you might find like-minded teachers you can turn to for trustworthy support as you push for significant change in your classroom or school. Could you get involved in and draw on any of the many small communities of educators within ASCD—such as ASCD's Affiliates or Professional Interest Communities, or the special interest groups that interact regularly on ASCD's social networking platform EDge?

EL Takeaways
On Being a Teacher

"In teaching, your effectiveness doesn't depend on your own efforts alone. It depends on how well you support and motivate your students."
— *Linda Darling-Hammond*

"Being flexible might be the most important thing teachers can "do" to help students who challenge us—in fact all students." — *Larry Ferlazzo*

"It's urgent to avoid mistakes in your first year teaching. The only other profession where it's more difficult to salvage your mistakes is tight-rope walking." — *Gary Rubinstein*

"It's crucial for veteran teachers and school leaders to build the infrastructure to support new teachers' success. Rookies don't grow into strong teachers if they're in hostile environments or under attack." — *Dan Brown*

"The role of a leader in education—whether that person is a teacher at heart, a *teacherpreneur*, or never was a teacher—must be to inspire and give space to teachers' problem-solving ability. This is a risk worth taking in education today." — *Ariel Sacks*

Related ASCD Resources

At the time of publication, the following ASCD resources were available (ASCD stock numbers appear in parentheses). For up-to-date information about ASCD resources, go to www.ascd.org. You can search the complete archives of *Educational Leadership* at http://www.ascd.org/el.

ASCD EDge®
Exchange ideas and connect with other educators interested in math on the social networking site ASCD EDge at http://ascdedge.ascd.org.

Print Products
Igniting Teacher Leadership: How do I empower my teachers to lead and learn? (ASCD Arias) by William Sterrett (#SF116039)

Intentional and Targeted Teaching: A Framework for Teacher Growth and Leadership by Douglas Fisher, Nancy Frey, and Stefani Hite (#116008)

Never Work Harder Than Your Students and Other Principles of Great Teaching by Robyn R. Jackson (#109001)

Qualities of Effective Teachers, 2nd Edition by James H. Stronge (#105156)

Starting School Right: How do I plan for a successful first week in my classroom? (ASCD Arias) by Otis Kriegel (#SF116009)

Teach, Reflect, Learn: Building Your Capacity for Success in the Classroom by Pete Hall and Alisa Simeral (#115040)

The New Teacher's Companion: Practical Wisdom for Succeeding in the Classroom by Gini Cunningham (#109051)

Where Great Teaching Begins: Planning for Student Thinking and Learning by Anne R. Reeves (#111023)

Educational Leadership, Dec 2015/Jan 2016: Co-Teaching: Making It Work (#116031)

Educational Leadership, May 2012: Supporting Beginning Teachers (#112023)

Educational Leadership, Dec 2010/Jan 2011: The Effective Educator (#111032)

PD Online® Courses
Building Teachers' Capacity for Success: Instructional Coaching Essentials (#PD15OC005M)

Where Great Teaching Begins: Designing Learning Objectives for Effective Instruction (#PD14OC017M)

For more information: send e-mail to member@ascd.org; call 1-800-933-2723 or 703-578-9600, press 2; send a fax to 703-575-5400; or write to Information Services, ASCD, 1703 N. Beauregard St., Alexandria, VA 22311-1714 USA.

ASCD's Whole Child approach is an effort to transition from a focus on narrowly defined academic achievement to one that promotes the long-term development and success of all children. Through this approach, ASCD supports educators, families, community members, and policymakers as they move from a vision about educating the whole child to sustainable, collaborative actions.

On Being a Teacher: Readings from Educational Leadership relates to the **engaged** and **supported** tenets.

WHOLE CHILD
TENETS

① HEALTHY
Each student enters school **healthy** and learns about and practices a healthy lifestyle.

② SAFE
Each student learns in an environment that is physically and emotionally **safe** for students and adults.

③ ENGAGED
Each student is actively **engaged** in learning and is connected to the school and broader community.

④ SUPPORTED
Each student has access to personalized learning and is **supported** by qualified, caring adults.

⑤ CHALLENGED
Each student is **challenged** academically and prepared for success in college or further study and for employment and participation in a global environment.

For more about the Whole Child approach, visit **www.wholechildeducation.org**.

www.ingramcontent.com/pod-product-compliance
Lightning Source LLC
Chambersburg PA
CBHW070626300426
44113CB00010B/1674